# The ISLAMIC MARY

# The ISLAMIC MARY

## Maryam Through the Centuries

YOUNUS Y. MIRZA

FORTRESS PRESS
Minneapolis

THE ISLAMIC MARY

Maryam Through the Centuries



30 29 28 27 26 25 2 3 4 5 6 7 8 9 10

Library of Congress Control Number: 2025932831 (print)

Cover image: Maryam (Mary) at the palm tree with baby ʻIsa (Jesus). From the Qisas al-anbiya (The Tales of the Prophets) by Ishaq ibn Ibrahim al-Nishapuri. Iran (probably Qazvin), c. 1570. Chester Beatty Library Per 231.227

Cover design: Brittany Becker

Print ISBN: 978-1-5064-8245-3

eBook ISBN: 978-1-5064-8246-0

# CONTENTS

# A NOTE TO THE READER

All Qur'anic translations are adapted from the work of M. A. S. Abdel Haleem.[1] I cite Qur'anic verses by the chapter number and verse, such as 3:42.

I frequently use Arabic names and phrases and often put them in parentheses as a reference. For Arabic words, I use the *International Journal for Middle Eastern Studies* (*IJMES*) style guide for transliteration; however, to make the text more accessible, I do not include diacritics.

When speaking about a biblical and Qur'anic figure in both traditions, I mention both names such as Abraham/Ibrahim. When referencing the biblical story, I use common English names such as Abraham. When writing about the figure in the Islamic tradition, I use the Qur'anic name such as Ibrahim. However, I use the name Maryam throughout to reference the Islamic Mary.

When mentioning a classical Muslim figure, I list the date they passed away in both the Islamic and Gregorian calendars, such as Ibn Kathir (d. 774/1373).

1. M. A. S. Abdel Haleem, trans., *The Qur'an* (Oxford University Press, 2008).

# PREFACE

## *The Personal Origins of This Book*

I was the only boy in my family with three sisters, a strong mother, and an encouraging dad. Growing up, I was always trying to get involved in my sisters' activities, to the point that their Girl Scout troop made me an honorary member. My mother was on the board of our local mosque and had us participate in its various fundraisers and programs. The mosque was trying to transition out of an office building, so I used to sell rugs and holiday cards to help build the new house of worship. My mother would eventually start her own nonprofit (one that I continue to be involved with), which helps orphans, refugees, and domestic violence survivors. Now, years later, I find history repeating itself as I am married to a strong woman and have three daughters of my own (and no sons). I am trying to figure out how to nurture my own children's identity with the weight of legacy and history and the demands of a modern lifestyle.

Women have always played a dominant role in my life, whether it be in my family, education, or workplace. They have been my caretakers, teachers, and mentors. However, when we look at history, women's voices and stories are not always represented, documented, or written about. This is especially true of Islamic studies, where there is a plethora of biographies of various male figures but few female ones.[1] Women are everywhere in the history of Islam, from early pioneers to the founders of endowments. In Muhammad's biography, for instance, we read of figures such as Khadija and ʻAyisha, his influential wives, and Fatima, his famous daughter. But other voices are not always represented or heard, and full-length monographs are rarely written about them.

1. For instance, the "Makers of the Muslim World" series from Oneworld has only two biographies dedicated to Muslim women out of a total of forty-six titles.

Moreover, my interest in biblical and Qur'anic figures emerges from my own name and family history. My grandfather grew up in what is now known as Pakistan and had an interest in prophetic names. He named his first child Isma'il (more commonly Ishmael in English), his second son Ibrahim (Abraham), his third Ishaq (Isaac), and his last, my father, Yaqub (Jacob). When my mother was pregnant with my older sister, my father asked my grandfather, "What should I name my child?" He responded that if the child was a girl, then he should name her Fatima, and if it was a boy, he should name him Younus (Jonah). My older sister was born, and I came a couple of years after. I did not know my grandfather that well because I was born in the United States, and he died when I was young. But my name always connects me to him, his legacy and story.

Growing up in the United States, I quickly realized that Younus was not a common name and that people had trouble pronouncing it. I was frequently the only Younus in my class or entire school. Many would correctly pronounce my name as *You-nus*, while others would say *Yo-nus* or *Ya-nis*. My football coach used to call me *YO-nus*, and I once corrected him, saying, "Coach, my name is *You-nus*, not *YO-nus*." He responded, "Don't worry, YO-nus. I'll get it right." I didn't correct him again. Having an "unusual" name made me curious about what it meant, its origins and history.

This personal history led me to my academic interests regarding the relationship between biblical and Qur'anic figures. Much of my research has focused on figures such as Abraham/Ibrahim, Moses/Musa, and Mary/Maryam, who are shared among Judaism, Christianity, and Islam, or (as they are often called) the Abrahamic religions.[2] My interests lie in how various texts interact, draw on one another, and eventually become canonized and form independent scriptures. Specifically, I examine the debates that emerged around biblical and Qur'anic figures and how the

2. For more discussion of the term *Abrahamic*, see Jon D. Levenson, *Inheriting Abraham: The Legacy of the Patriarch in Judaism, Christianity, and Islam* (Princeton University Press, 2012); Carol Bakhos, *The Family of Abraham: Jewish, Christian, and Muslim Interpretations* (Harvard University Press, 2014).

discussions not only represent the figures themselves but also represent the communities that hold them to be relevant and sacred. Whether it is defining which child Abraham/Ibrahim attempted to sacrifice or who Musa's father-in-law was, these debates often occur because of scriptural silence, interdependence, and ambiguity. However, when it comes to Maryam, scripture is not silent, with an entire chapter named after her.[3] Her story is thus heard but understood in different ways across time and space.

I became increasingly interested in Maryam after cowriting *The Bible and the Qur'an: Biblical Figures in the Islamic Tradition* with John Kaltner. In that book, we discuss forty-eight figures and groups that are shared among the scriptures, first by examining similarities and differences, and then exploring how they are received within the Islamic "Stories of the Prophets" (*qisas al-anbiya'*) literature. My primary role was to write the reception history of these figures and how they were understood in later Muslim literature. During my writing and research, I was fascinated by how Muslim authors expanded on the Qur'anic figures and added interesting details and anecdotes from Jewish and Christian sources. Such cross-pollination demonstrates that interreligious learning and comparative scripture are not only a modern phenomenon but occurred throughout history. However, later Muslim scholars would be skeptical of such interreligious approaches, as they felt it distracted from the Qur'anic and prophetic message.[4] With Maryam specifically, I was fascinated to learn about her story within Muslim life and literature, with many of these stories and debates largely unknown. I witnessed beautiful paintings of Maryam's life and learned about debates regarding her prophecy. Many of these discussions have been overlooked, and what has been written has not been given the prominence it deserves.

---

3. As we will discuss, scripture is silent over whether Maryam was a prophet, and thus a debate emerged regarding that issue.

4. Younus Y. Mirza, "Ishmael as Abraham's Sacrifice: Ibn Taymiyya and Ibn Kathir on the Intended Victim," *Islam and Christian–Muslim Relations* 24, no. 3 (2013): 277–298.

Last, the book represents my college experience, one where I went to a Jesuit and Catholic institution of Georgetown and learned about theology, religion, and Christianity. The university had a theology requirement, and I enjoyed taking the course The Problem of God and discussing theological issues across religious traditions. I remember students beginning to cry in class when we spoke about death and the professor explaining about how they went about writing and publication. I also had the opportunity to take Introduction to Biblical Literature and learned about many of the Qur'anic figures from a biblical perspective and how they fit within the world of Judaism and Christianity. I was surprised to learn how many of the figures were shared among religious traditions, such as the story of Joseph/Yusuf, who was also in the Bible. Along the way, I not only learned about Judaism and Christianity but also had Jewish and Christian friends, teachers, and mentors whom I continue to be in touch with and meet for advice and camaraderie. These relationships represent friendship and also a continuous learning opportunity, where I hear and learn from their unique perspectives, views, and ideas.

I was also in college when 9/11 occurred. I was a sophomore taking an Arabic class when one of the students walked in and asked, "Do you know what happened?" Before the rest of the students could respond, she declared "We've been attacked!" Class was immediately canceled, and I remember going to a fellow student's dorm room, where I watched the planes hitting the Twin Towers. We didn't fully comprehend what was happening, but I heard one of the students scream, "We have to bomb Hamas!" as they sought to decipher who the attacker was and how to retaliate. I still hoped that it was somehow an accident rather than a terrorist attack as I ran out of the dorm room, trying to get home. Leaving Washington, DC—the site of the second attack, on the Pentagon—was a mess with traffic jams and delays as folks attempted to evacuate the city. The cell phone towers were jammed, making it impossible to call home, but I eventually made it there several hours later. I remember walking on campus later that week, thinking how people might perceive me differently now because of my name and dark skin. My house of worship was vandalized with obscenities sprayed all over it and statements such as "Go Home" written prominently all over.

The attacks led to renewed calls of a "clash of civilizations" paradigm, where Islam was at war with the West, especially after the fall of the Soviet Empire. The years ahead would lead to a rise of Islamophobia, with informants, raids on Muslim communities, and religious and racial profiling. However, the events also led to increased outreach on the behalf of Muslim and non-Muslim communities, such as interfaith gatherings, open houses, and civic engagement. Greater society, including government and nonprofit organizations, also realized it needed to invest in better understanding Islam and Muslim culture. I was a beneficiary, receiving several scholarships to study Arabic in the United States and Middle East, and eventually joined an Arabic and Islamic Studies PhD program (also at Georgetown) that was newly formed. As a sophomore, I was still trying to figure out my major, but the events of 9/11 propelled me into a career of teaching, scholarship, and research, with the aim of better explaining Islam and Muslims and with the hope of building stronger bridges of understanding and peace.[5]

5. I often share with students the story of 9/11 and my college experiences so they can reflect on how the larger social and political events may affect their careers and future goals and aspirations.

# INTRODUCTION

I belong to the 9/11 generation that grew up in the '90s but came of age in the early 2000s and witnessed war, conflict, and religious misunderstanding. I remember being a boy when the Persian Gulf War started and the first images were broadcast on cable news. I participated in rallies to end the genocide in Bosnia and helped Bosnian refugees relocate here in the United States. I was a student at Georgetown University when 9/11 happened and felt the impact of the event on my life and career.

During this time, a renewed emphasis on the "clash of civilizations" thesis appeared. In 1993, Samuel Huntington famously declared that one of the next threats after the fall of communism would be the "green" threat instead of the communist "red" one. According to Huntington, the next conflicts would be between civilizations with similar histories, cultures, and religions. He believed that "the next world war, if there is one, will be a war between civilizations."[1] In this new world, it would be the "West versus the rest," and Western civilization needed to bond together and quell internal strife to thwart external threats and nemeses. Within this scheme, "Islam" had its own civilization and provided a potential threat to the West alongside the "Confucian" civilization of China. As Huntington famously stated, "Islam had bloody borders," and there was a historic and intrinsic conflict between "Islam and the West."[2]

1. Samuel Huntington, "The Clash of Civilizations?" *Foreign Affairs* 72, no. 3 (1993): 29.

2. See also his subsequent book, Samuel Huntington, *The Clash of Civilizations and the Remaking of World Order* (Simon and Schuster, 1996). For responses and critiques to

But a counternarrative developed that a conflict between Islam and the West was not inevitable and that the various civilizations and religions could live in peace and coexistence.[3] This narrative built on previous intellectual efforts that saw Abraham/Ibrahim as a common figure among Judaism, Christianity, and Islam who could unite the various religious traditions in an age of war and conflict. The great religions shared scripture, ethics, and the idea of monotheism and overlapped in terms of values and culture. Some even suggested that the modern conflicts were akin to a family feud or sibling rivalry, as the different religions returned to the same father, Abraham, and were part of a larger family.

However, a series of books emerged critiquing this shared notion of Abraham/Ibrahim and how he was portrayed in public discourse as well as interfaith and interreligious circles.[4] The authors admitted that Abraham was "shared" among various religions but that they understood him in different ways and within their own theology and religious understandings. The various attempts at Abrahamic religions often glossed over these differences and, at times, suggested creating a new religion rather than respecting the multiple traditions and their unique histories.[5] While global peace and understanding among the

---

this narrative, see Emran Qureshi and Michael Anthony Sells, eds., *The New Crusades: Constructing the Muslim Enemy* (Columbia University Press, 2003).

3. Bruce S. Feiler, *Abraham: A Journey to the Heart of Three Faiths* (W. Morrow, 2002); F. E. Peters, *The Children of Abraham: Judaism, Christianity, Islam* (Princeton University Press, 2004).

4. Levenson, *Inheriting Abraham*; Bakhos, *The Family of Abraham*; Aaron W. Hughes, *Abrahamic Religions: On the Uses and Abuses of History* (Oxford University Press, 2012).

5. As Jon Levenson concludes his book, "Rather than inventing a neutral Abraham to whom these three ancient communities must now hold themselves accountable, we would be better served by appreciating better both the profound commonalities and equally profound differences among them and why the commonalities and the differences alike have endured and show every sign of continuing to do so" (Levenson, *Inheriting Abraham*, 214). Nonetheless, I agree with Bakhos that "as fraught and imperfect as the term may be, on a practical level, it serves as shorthand for referring to

world religions is a noble idea, creating a "neutral Abraham" could do more harm than good and potentially generate more misunderstanding and mistrust.

While the term *Abrahamic* still holds currency, new books have emerged discussing the Islamic Mary or Maryam.[6] These books build on the ecumenical spirit of the early discussions on Abraham but highlight a new figure who opens innovative possibilities regarding Christian-Muslim relations, spirituality, and women and religion. Whereas Abraham represents the classic patriarch with his sons Ishmael/Isma'il and Isaac/Ishaq "fathering" the great religions of Judaism, Christianity, and Islam, Maryam represents a woman, a mother, and a spiritual figure who has inspired millions throughout the centuries.

The emphasis on Maryam also highlights the importance of Christian-Muslim relations in the world today and in the future. According to a Pew Poll, Christians and Muslims will be roughly the same number by 2050 and make up over half the world's population. As the 2007 *A Common Word* letter begins, "Without peace and justice between these two religious communities, there can be no meaningful peace in the world. The future of the world depends on peace between Muslims and Christians."[7] In other words, international peace is highly dependent on peace between Christians and Muslims, and their interaction will have global consequences. Yet this scholarly emphasis on Maryam is aware of the critiques made against Abraham and Abrahamic religions and largely avoids trying to create a "neutral Mary" but instead seeks to better understand how she operates in the different religions.

---

Judaism, Christianity, and Islam. This purpose is especially useful when highlighting commonalities" (Bakhos, *The Family of Abraham*, 7).

6. Hosn Abboud, *Mary in the Qur'an: A Literary Reading* (Routledge / Taylor and Francis, 2014); Rita George Tvrtković, *Christians, Muslims, and Mary: A History* (Paulist Press, 2018); Muna Tatari and Klaus von Stosch, *Mary in the Qur'an: Friend of God, Virgin, Mother*, trans. Peter Lewis (Gingko, 2021).

7. The Royal Aal Al-Bayt Institute for Islamic Thought, *A Common Word: Between Us and You* (Al Manhal, 2013).

Thus, within this backdrop, I begin this book on the Islamic Mary or Maryam. Like those before, I seek to better understand Maryam in the Islamic tradition, hoping she can be a source of religious history, ecumenism, and spirituality.[8] Nonetheless, unlike other works, I don't only look at her through the Qur'an but also examine how she appears throughout history, such as within prophetic reports, theology, mysticism, art, and modernity. In many ways, the Qur'anic portrayals motivate various Muslim engagements with Maryam throughout time and place, up until the contemporary period. Maryam continues to inspire Muslim communities, with her name given to daughters, her Qur'anic chapter read in mosques, and her story shared in countless classes and sermons. But her history is still just beginning to be explored, and her full potential is just starting to be realized.

8. Aliah Schleifer, *Mary the Blessed Virgin of Islam* (Fons Vitae, 2008).

CHAPTER ONE

# Maryam in the Qur'an

MARYAM IS FREQUENTLY subsumed under Jesus/'Isa and is not seen as a figure in her own right. However, the most authoritative scripture in Islam, the Qur'an, presents Maryam as a protagonist, extols her spiritual state, and places her within its worldview.[1] In this chapter, I focus on how Maryam fits within the Qur'an's framework of a daughter, spiritual role model, and mother. The Qur'anic depiction of Mary helps us better understand not only the figure of Maryam in the Islamic tradition but also how Islam views God, righteousness, comfort, and despair.

## Daughters in the Qur'an

Writings on Maryam in the Qur'an often begin with verses that deal directly with her, such as those that speak about her birth and the annunciation of 'Isa. However, to properly appreciate these verses, we must understand them from within the context of the Qur'an in general and specifically how it discusses daughters and mothers.[2]

The Qur'an describes how the pre-Islamic Arabs shunned daughters and would frown and become upset at their birth. These verses are often found within the context of Qur'anic discussions of Islamic monotheism, which assert that God is absolute, unique, and thus without a family. This monotheistic position contrasts with that of the pre-Islamic

1. Another article that makes a similar point is Hosn Abboud, "Is Mary Important for Herself or for Being the Mother of Christ in the Holy Qur'an?" *Al-Raida* 125 (2009): 26–36.

2. For a more extensive discussion of Qur'anic daughters, see Celene Ibrahim, *Women and Gender in the Qur'an* (Oxford University Press, 2020).

Arab pagans, who held that God had daughters, even though they were ashamed themselves of their own female offspring. The Qur'an indicates that female infanticide was a common outcome of such embarrassment: "When one of them is given news of the birth of a baby girl, his face darkens and he is filled with gloom. In his shame, he hides himself away from his people because of the bad news he has been given. Should he keep her and suffer humiliation or bury her in the dust? How evil they judge!" (Q. 16:58–59).[3]

In this passage the Qur'an describes the birth of a female child as a "glad tiding" (*bashshara*), a verb used in the Qur'an to indicate a multitude of blessings. Commentators explain that the term *glad tiding* (*tabshir*) "is related to news that should lead to happiness."[4] The word is further connected to one's facial "complexion" and suggests that one's face should change to the positive once hearing the news. The term is frequently used in the Qur'an in reference to male and female children, paradise, nature, and believers. For instance, the word is used regarding the glad tidings of paradise (2:25), the reward of the patient (2:155), and belief (2:223). The believers on the day of judgment will laugh and rejoice (*mustabshira*) at the good news of them attaining paradise. The wind is a glad tiding as it brings the rain, pushes the boats, and changes the seasons (25:48; 30:46). Muhammad, as well as the messengers in general, are frequently referred to as ones who bring glad tidings (*mubashshir*). Moreover, various Qur'anic messengers and figures are given the glad tidings of offspring, many of whom become prophets themselves. For instance, Ibrahim and Sarah are given the glad tidings of Ishaq's birth (11:71), even in their old age. Moreover, Zachariah/Zakariyya is given the good news of John the Baptist/Yahya (3:39), and Maryam is given the glad tidings that she will give birth to 'Isa (3:45).

---

3. All the translations in this book are adapted from M. A. S. Abdel Haleem, trans., *The Qur'an*(Oxford University Press, 2008).

4. Fakhr al-Din al-Razi, *al-Tafsir al-kabir*, ed. Sayyid 'Umran, 32 vols. (Dar al-Hadith, 2012), 10: 264.

However, the man described in Q. 16:58–59 does not see his daughter as a "glad tiding" but rather as a humiliation.[5] He is full of grief and contemplates whether he should live with the embarrassment or bury her alive. The Qur'an unequivocally condemns this behavior by stating, "How evil is what they judge!"[6] The following verses further use the word *evil*: "To those who disbelieve in the Hereafter belong all evil qualities, whereas to Allah belong the finest attributes. And He is the Almighty, All-Wise" (16:60). The verse implies that female infanticide is a problem of the absence of faith and disbelief in the hereafter.[7]

Regarding Q. 16:58–59, Qur'anic commentators assert that female infanticide is a spiritual problem, wherein one rejects the decree of God. The famous Sufi Qur'anic exegete al-Qushayri (d. 465/1072–73) explains that female infanticide is a symptom of hardening the heart and expresses dismay over killing a child who has no sin. The traditionalist exegete al-Tabari (d. 310/923) notes that female infanticide is an example of rejecting the divine will by not accepting the gender of the child at birth. He argues that the "believer is content with what God decrees for them. The decree of God is better than the decree of a person for themselves. For one's life, [God knows] which one (a male or female) child is better. A daughter may be better for her family than a son."[8] Moreover, the Qur'anic commentaries preserve a tradition where

5. The Qur'an also uses the word *bashshara* in a sarcastic way in reference to announcing the punishment of hellfire to disbelievers.

6. This section of the verse could also refer to pre-Islamic Arabs' decision to attribute daughters to God.

7. Donna Lee Bowen, "Infanticide," in *Encyclopaedia of the Qur'ān*, ed. Jane Dammen McAuliffe (E. J. Brill, 2021). For instance, Asma Barlas states, "The Qur'an not only condemns female infanticide and the abuse of daughters, but it also promises that on Judgement Day, God will question 'the female (infant) buried alive . . . for what crime she was killed.' (On that day, when sons will not avail fathers, a baby girl's testimony will seal her father's fate!) There is thus no question that the Qur'an does not give fathers the right to kill or maltreat their daughters." Asma Barlas, "The Qur'an and Hermeneutics: Reading the Qur'an's Opposition to Patriarchy," *Journal of Qur'anic Studies* 3, no. 2 (2001): 15–38.

8. Abu Ja'far Muhammad b. Jarir al-Tabari, *Jami' al-bayan fi tafsir al-Qur'an*, ed. 'Abdullah b. 'Abd al-Muhsin al-Turki, 26 vols. (Dar al-Hijr, 2001), 14: 256.

the companion Qays b. ʿAsim admitted to the Prophet Muhammad that he had buried his daughters alive in pre-Islamic times (*jahiliyya*). The Prophet Muhammad then ordered him, "Free a slave for each one [that you killed]." The man explains that he did not have slaves but was a camel owner. The Prophet Muhammad then responds, "You should slaughter a grown camel for each one [you killed]."[9] The tradition demonstrates that the Prophet Muhammad still demanded expiation for the crime of female infanticide even though it occurred before the companion came to Islam.[10]

In another set of verses, the Qur'an describes the end of time, such as when the sun dims, the stars fall, and the mountains are blown away. At this apocalyptic ending, the Qur'an asks, "And when baby girls, buried alive, are asked: for what crime were they killed?" (81:8–9). The verses suggest that on the day of judgment, the crime of female infanticide will be questioned and those guilty held accountable.[11] While the dominant reading of this verse is of the baby girl being asked rhetorically why she has been killed, the Qur'anic commentaries preserve a variant recitation (*sa'alat* instead of *su'ilat*) where the infant directly asks her murderer, "What sin was I killed for?" In this reading, the daughter is the one asking, rather than being asked, why she was murdered.

Beyond the Qur'an's condemnation of female infanticide, there is strong evidence of the role of daughters in the text. Indeed, "the Qur'an does not depict a corrupt daughter figure, nor any instance of a parent who has a strained relationship with a daughter."[12] For instance, essential daughter figures emerge in the story of Musa, especially in helping

9. Ibn Kathir, *Tafsir al-Qur'an al-ʿAzim*, ed. Sami Muhammad al-Salama, 8 vols. (Dar Tayyiba, 1998), 8: 334. Ibn Kathir notes that some narrations state that Qays had killed eight or twelve to thirteen daughters in pre-Islamic times.

10. It also demonstrates the connection between repentance for murder and emancipation of slaves.

11. As Avner Giladi explains, infanticide for both males and females was practiced among pre-Islamic Arabs but was more frequently implemented on females. Avner Giladi, "Some Observations on Infanticide in Medieval Muslim Society," *International Journal of Middle East Studies* 22 (1990): 186.

12. Ibrahim, *Women and Gender in the Qur'an*, 79.

save his life and in times of need. For example, after Musa's mom puts him in the Nile, she sends her daughter—Musa's sister—to follow him and make sure he is safe. The daughter then follows her brother from a distance while the palace guardsmen are unaware. When Musa is picked up at Pharaoh's palace, he refuses to suckle with any of the women, leading the daughter to say, "Shall I direct you to a family who will bring him up for you and take good care of him?" (28:12). The palace eventually consents, and Musa is returned to his mother and raised by her. The daughter (and sister of Musa) thus plays a crucial role in his safety and well-being and his return to his family.

Later in the story, Musa flees Egypt and arrives in the city of Midian dejected, isolated, and in need. He then sees the daughters of Jethro attempting to water their flock, but they are unable to do so because the city's men are preventing them. Despite being a refugee and stranger, Musa bravely intervenes and helps the women accomplish their task. This noble effort leads Musa to receive an invitation from Jethro himself after the daughters explain to him what happened. Musa accepts the invitation and shares his story and predicament with the family. Jethro comforts Musa by telling him not to be afraid and that he is safe; he has been rescued from the unjust. One of Jethro's daughters then asks her father to hire Musa because he is "strong" and "trustworthy"; Musa eventually marries one of Jethro's daughters and works with him and his family for eight years.[13]

In summary, the Qur'an affirms the birth of daughters, condemns those who kill them, and sees their birth as a glad tiding and blessing. Daughters further play a positive role in the Qur'an by helping those in need and providing advice and support when necessary.

## Maryam as a Qur'anic Daughter

It is within this Qur'anic backdrop that we must first understand Maryam as a daughter rather than a mother, specifically the mother

13. For more on the debates within this story, see Younus Y. Mirza, "Ibn Taymiyya as Exegete: Moses' Father-in-Law and the Messengers in Sūrat Yā Sīn," *Journal of Qur'anic Studies* 19 (2017): 39–71.

of ʻIsa. Both Christians and Muslims frequently emphasize Mary/Maryam's maternal qualities and background, but the Qur'an does not initially introduce her as such. Rather than as a mother, she is first introduced as the daughter of Anna/Hana (*imratu ʿImran* / the wife of ʿImran).[14] This distinction is significant because Mary's birth is not discussed in the canonical Bible, which instead first highlights the annunciation of Jesus. Rather, noncanonical sources, like the Protoevangelium of James, speak about Mary's birth in a similar way to the Qur'an.[15] However, even the Protoevangelium of James does not note Hana's surprise when she gives birth to a female and the potential disappointment that it could have caused.

The Qur'an begins the story of Maryam with her mother, identified as Hana in the Islamic tradition, vowing that whatever is in her womb will be dedicated to God and his service: "Lord, I have dedicated what is growing in my womb entirely to You; so accept this from me. You are the One who hears and knows all" (3:35).[16] However, instead of a boy who would be more readily accepted among the priestly class, she gives birth to a girl, leading to dismay: "But when she gave birth, she said, 'My Lord! I have given birth to a girl.'"[17] In the echoes of Hana's voice,

14. Modern scholars frequently date the chapter of Maryam (19) as before the verses in the chapter of Al ʿImran (3). However, in terms of the order of the text, the verses in the chapter of Al ʿImran come first. Angelika Neuwirth, "Mary and Jesus: Counterbalancing the Biblical Patriarchs: A Re-Reading of Sūrat Maryam in Sūrat Āl ʿImrān (Q. 3:1–62)," in *Scripture, Poetry, and the Making of a Community: Reading the Qur'an as a Literary Text*, ed. Angelika Neuwirth (Oxford University Press, 2014), 359–384.

15. Rita George-Tvrtkovič, *Christians, Muslims, and Mary: A History* (Paulist Press, 2018), 5.

16. As Saritoprak explains, "The Qur'anic story of Mary can be divided roughly into three parts: her family and mother up to her birth, her early life, and her adulthood which includes the story of her giving birth to Jesus." The first part of the story, or "her family and mother up to her birth," is frequently overlooked to emphasize the birth of Jesus. Zeki Saritoprak, "Mary in Islam," in *The Oxford Handbook of Mary*, ed. Chris Maunder (Oxford University Press, 2019), 94.

17. Qur'anic verse 3:36.

we perhaps hear the voices of the other Qur'anic verses where parents were disappointed in the birth of a daughter, leading them to bury her alive or live with her in humiliation.

However, once again, the Qur'an affirms the birth of daughters even if one had expected a boy. The divine voice of the Qur'an affirms the birth of the female, acknowledging God's omnipotence and omniscience: "God knew best what she had given birth to: the male is not like the female."[18] Moreover, instead of rejecting her daughter, as many pre-Islamic Arab parents had done, Hana accepts her, works to fulfill her vow, names her, and prays for her protection: "I name her Maryam and I commend her and her offspring to Your protection from the rejected Satan." The Qur'an then shares that "her Lord graciously accepted her and made her grow in goodness" and that the prophet Zakariyya was entrusted to care for her. Commenting on these verses, Zeki Saritoprak explains, "On the surface, it seems that as Maryam's mother was expecting a boy and she gave birth to a girl, her prayer was not accepted; however, as the Qur'an states, her prayer was accepted in the most beautiful way. God accepted her earlier prayer when Maryam was born and her later prayer after Maryam was born. Thus, both she and her offspring were protected from the touch of Satan."[19] God did accept Hana's prayer even though she did not realize it at first.[20]

18. As *The Study Qur'an* states, "One way to understanding 'the male is not like the female' is that it establishes that there are real, meaningful differences between the sexes; at the same time, however, God accepted her with a beautiful acceptance' suggesting that those differences are irrelevant from the spiritual point of view." Seyyed Hossein Nasr et al., eds., *The Study Quran: A New Translation and Commentary* (HarperOne, 2015), 141.

19. Saritoprak, "Mary in Islam," 94.

20. Similarly, as Leyla Ozgur Alhassen explains, "God has blessed Maryam and her child, just as her mother had prayed. This shows that Maryam's mother's fears about having a girl were unfounded. Just as the audience is deliberately left ignorant of important facts, so too are the characters in the story mistaken in some of their assumptions and fears." Leyla Ozgur Alhassen, *Qur'anic Stories: God, Revelation and the Audience* (Edinburgh University Press, 2021), 24.

A Qur'anic emphasis on Maryam as a daughter also appears elsewhere in the text. The Qur'an frequently refers to Mary as "Maryam" and to 'Isa as the "son of Maryam." However, there are instances when Maryam is referred to as a "daughter" and not just in association with 'Isa. For instance, the Qur'an states, "Mary, *daughter* of 'Imran. She guarded her chastity, so We breathed into her from Our spirit. She accepted the truth of her Lord's words and Scriptures: she was truly devout" (66:12). This verse appears in the context of a comparison of disbelieving and righteous women. Here, the Qur'an ends the section and chapter by discussing Maryam as the "daughter of 'Imran." She is praised as being chaste, close to God, and existing among the devout. While the other women mentioned in this section are referred to as the "wives" of their husbands, Maryam is the only one referred to as a "daughter," highlighting the significance of the title and honorific. The Qur'an further ends the chapter highlighting the example of Maryam that speaks to earlier Qur'anic references that she is the "best woman of all time." The verse suggests that other women, such as the wives of the Prophet Muhammad, should follow her example and be among the "devout." Therefore, Maryam should not be seen simply as the mother of Jesus but also as the daughter of Anna/Hana and part of the family of 'Imran.

## Maryam Among the Spiritual Elite

The Qur'an does not speak of Maryam only in relationship to Jesus or her parents but also presents her as exhibiting her own spiritual insights, miracles, and personal struggles. When she is entrusted in the care of Zakariyya, he notices that she has been given provisions. This leads Zakariyya to ask, "Maryam, how is it you have these provisions?" to which she replies, "They are from God: God provides limitlessly for whoever He wills" (3:38). Even though Zakariyya had been delegated to take care of Maryam, it appears that God was already taking care of Maryam all along. Maryam here provides Zakariyya with an important spiritual lesson: "God provides limitlessly for whoever He wills."[21] Zakariyya then understands from Maryam that if she can receive provisions from God, then he could also receive anything. He then prays to God for the birth of a child, and God responds that he will have a son. Thus, Maryam's example leads to Zakariyya's prayer, which ultimately leads to the birth of Yahya, one of the supporters and forerunners of 'Isa.[22]

The verses continue with the angels saying, "Maryam, God has chosen you and made you pure: He has truly chosen you above all women" (3:42). The Qur'anic verse speaks directly to Maryam, demonstrating that she is an immediate recipient of the divine voice of the Qur'an. Moreover, the Arabic word here for *chosen* (*istafa*) is frequently used to describe God "choosing" prophets, leading some Qur'anic commentators to believe that Maryam was herself a prophet.[23] Muhammad is often described as the *chosen one* (*mustafa*), and several verses earlier in the chapter state that "God chose (*istafa*) Adam, Noah, Abraham's family, and the family of 'Imran, over all other people" (3:33). The phrase "He has truly chosen you above all women" was further debated among Qur'anic exegetes. Did Maryam rank above women of her time or for *all* times? Many Muslim scholars, such as the famous medieval scholar Ibn Kathir (d. 774/1373), held that Maryam was the best woman, even

---

21. As Alhassen notes, "The phrasing in Maryam's words is almost exactly the same as an earlier verse in which a second-person addressee is told to say to God: 'You provide limitlessly for whoever You will' *tarzuqu man tasha' bi-ghayri hisab* (3:27). Maryam's words echoing the earlier phrase show the strength of her faith, and that she says exactly what God tells people to say. Here, then, once again we see how much God has blessed her, which is what Maryam's mother had wanted. Maryam's words submit to God's words." Alhassen, *Qur'anic Stories*, 24.

22. John Kaltner and Younus Mirza, *The Bible and the Quran: Biblical Figures in the Islamic Tradition* (Bloomsbury Academic, 2018), 94. Scholars have noticed the close association between Maryam and Zachariah/Zakariyya and then Jesus/'Isa and John/Yahya in the Qur'an. Barbara Stowasser, "Mary," in *Encyclopaedia of the Qur'ān*, ed. Jane Dammen McAuliffe (E. J. Brill, 2021).

23. Younus Y. Mirza, "The Islamic Mary: Between Prophecy and Orthodoxy," *Journal of Qur'anic Studies* 23, no. 3 (2021): 70–102.

better than Muhammad's wife Khadija and daughter Fatima. However, others, especially those in the Shi'i tradition, held that Maryam was second only to Fatima.[24]

Particularly striking in these Qur'anic verses is the direct communication that Maryam receives from God, with many commentators believing the angel speaking to her was Gabriel/Jibril. Angels similarly speak directly to Maryam about the birth of her child: "The angels said, 'Maryam, God gives you news of a Word from Him, whose name will be the Messiah, Jesus, son of Maryam, who will be held in honor in this world and the next, who will be one of those brought near to God'" (3:45). The Qur'an captures Maryam's surprise by stating, "My Lord, how can I have a son when no man has touched me?" This leads the angel to declare, "This is how God creates what He will: when He has ordained something, He only says, 'Be', and it is" (3:47). 'Isa's birth is understood to be a miracle and part of God's limitless ability. Qur'anic commentators further picked up on the fact that Maryam did not ask for a sign, unlike Zakariyya. She accepts the divine will and puts her trust in God, leading some to rank her above the prophet.[25]

This direct divine communication is repeated in the chapter of Maryam (19), where the Qur'an now speaks of the angel as a "human being" and a "spirit." In this section, Maryam fears that the man is there to harm her: "I seek the Lord of Mercy's protection against you: if you have any fear of Him [do not approach]!" (19:18). However, the messenger comforts Maryam, explaining, "I am but a Messenger from your Lord, [come] to announce to you the gift of a pure son" (19:19). She once again responds in astonishment but this time emphasizes her

24. Jane D. McAuliffe, "'Chosen Among All Women': Mary and Fatima in Qur'anic Exegesis," *Islamochristiana* 7 (1981): 19–28; Mary F. Thurlkill, *Chosen Among Women: Mary and Fatima in Medieval Christianity and Shi'ite Islam* (University of Notre Dame Press, 2008). As Stowasser explains, "The problem is addressed by questioning whether Mary's preeminence is absolute (over all other women and for all times) or relative (over the women of her own time)." Stowasser, "Mary." For potential biblical parallels for these verses, see Gabriel Said Reynolds, *The Qur'an and the Bible: Text and Commentary* (Yale University Press, 2018), 118–120.

25. For more on this discussion, see Mirza, "The Islamic Mary."

chastity: "How can I have a son when no man has touched me? I have not been unchaste!" (19:20).[26] The angel once more assures Maryam and asserts God's miracle: "This is what your Lord said: 'It is easy for Me—We shall make him a sign to all people, a blessing from Us'. And so, it was ordained: she conceived him" (19:21). The verse ends reemphasizing God's omnipotence and ability to do whatever He wills.

## Maryam's Labor and the Birth of 'Isa

The Qur'an describes Maryam's labor, which contrasts with the Bible and fits within the larger Qur'anic framework of acknowledging mothers' pain in giving birth and work in nursing.[27] In the story of Maryam's childbirth, she withdraws "to a distant place," suggesting that she is alone and isolated and going through this trial by herself. In contrast, the biblical story describes Maryam with Elizabeth or the wife of Zakariyya. In the Qur'an, her isolation demonstrates her total dependence on God as she goes through the birth by herself.[28] As the pangs of labor arrive, she cries out, "I wish I had been dead and forgotten long before this!" (19:23).

Commentators have long debated the meaning of this potentially blasphemous phrase: Was Maryam rejecting the divine decree in giving birth?[29] Maryam had seemed to accept God's command when the angel

26. As *The Study Qur'an* states, "Mary's response is understood to be an inquiry as to how the conception of the child would come about, for example, through marriage to someone or in another way, rather than an expression of doubt regarding the message the angel has brought." Nasr et al., *The Study Qur'an*, 769.

27. As Hosn Abboud notes, "Even though Mary's story in the sura of Mary is about childbirth, it is primarily her story. The events revolve around her, and the characters converse with her because of who she is in herself." Hosn Abboud, "'Idhan Maryam Nabiyya' ['Hence Maryam Is a Prophetess']: Muslim Classical Exegetes and Women's Receptiveness to God's Verbal Inspiration," in *Mariam, the Magdalen, and the Mother*, ed. Deirdre Joy Good (Indiana University Press, 2005), 35.

28. George-Tvrtković, *Christians, Muslims, and Mary*, 11.

29. For instance, Maria Dakake, in *The Study Qur'an*, notes that "al-Razi observes that longing for death is often the response of the righteous to suffering, as they refuse to

appeared, but does she now wish for death?[30] This statement is unique to the Qur'an; in the Bible, "Mary does not complain; instead, she sings a song of praise, the Magnificat: "My soul magnifies the Lord" (Luke 1:46–55)."[31] Some scholars have "speculated that Mary was reacting to the shame that the birth of a child out of wedlock would bring upon her family and their honor. According to such interpretations, death would be a lesser evil than the possibility of dishonoring herself and her family."[32] In this reading, Maryam wished death upon herself because of the potential shame she would cause herself and her family for having a child without a husband. However, such a reading is suspect because Maryam does not voice such a concern when the angel first approaches her. Why would she only be concerned about her honor when she was about to give birth and not before?

A more plausible answer is that Maryam cries out when she begins to feel the pain of childbirth, which is consistent with the Qur'anic

---

abandon their moral or spiritual duties, but are nonetheless fearful of or saddened by the consequences that may result . . . On a spiritual level, Mary's statement can be understood as expressing the ultimate victory against the worldly ego, for it indicates that she wished not only to withdraw from and forget the world, but also to be utterly forgotten by it," 770.

30. As Rita George-Tvrtković notes, "Another interesting difference between the birth stories is the Qur'an, where Mary is described as delivering Jesus under a palm tree and is miraculously provided with dates to eat (19:22–25). Neither the Bible nor the Protoevangelium mentions a palm tree or dates, but these details can be found in other Christian apocryphal texts like the *Infancy Gospel of Thomas*, the *Gospel of Pseudo-Matthew*, the *Apocryphal Gospel of Matthew*, and the *Book of Mary's Repose*." George-Tvrtković, *Christians, Muslims, and Mary*, 11.

31. George-Tvrtković, *Christians, Muslims, and Mary*, 2.

32. Asma Sayeed, "Mary," in *The Oxford Encyclopedia of the Islamic World*, ed. John Esposito (Oxford University Press, 2021). Zeki Saritoprak states that in verse 19:23, "her frustration is understandable. This is a woman of chastity and honour and such a woman with such an important place in her society is now facing a social dilemma. She is unable to explain her situation, a situation which had never before happened" (Saritoprak, "Mary in Islam," 96). However, I read this section as Mary complaining about the labor pains, not necessarily being concerned here about the reaction of her people, which only comes later. Such a reading corresponds with the larger Qur'anic narrative that emphasizes labor pains and travails of mothers.

verses that speak about the challenges of motherhood, specifically pregnancy and labor. For instance, the Qur'an states, "We have commanded people to be good to their parents: their mothers carried them, with strain upon strain, and it takes two years to wean them. Give thanks to Me and to your parents—all will return to Me" (31:14). Here, gratitude is connected to both God and one's parents, especially mothers because of the toil spent giving birth and raising children. In a similar verse, the Qur'an states, "We have commanded humanity to be good to their parents: their mother struggled to carry them and struggled to give birth to him" (46:15). In this verse, labor is mentioned explicitly alongside pregnancy as a form of struggle that a mother goes through and a reason children should be good to their parents. Commenting on these verses, some exegetes observe that the Qur'an makes a general proclamation to be good to one's parents but specifically mentions the struggles and hardships of mothers. One commentator even states that these verses "indicate that [the mother's] rights are more," and various prophetic traditions support this.[33] Modern scholars also note that in the Qur'an, "the role of mothers—women who conceive, give *birth* and sustain infants through the period of lactation—is noted with respect. Muslims are commanded to 'honor the mothers that bore you' (4:1) and to show kindness to parents."[34]

Nonetheless, to explain Maryam's statement, some commentators note that wishing for death "is the habit of the righteous that if they find themselves in a tribulation, then they say such things."[35] The commentator al-Razi gives the example of the Battle of the Camel, where 'Ali, the fourth caliph and cousin of the Prophet Muhammad, would face the army of 'Ayisha, the wife of the Prophet Muhammad. Before the battle, he states, "I wish I had died twenty years before this." Similarly, the caliph 'Umar once picked up a straw on the earth and empathized with it, lamenting,

33. al-Razi, *al-Tafsir al-kabir*, 14: 281.

34. Donna Lee Bowen, "Birth," in *Encyclopaedia of the Qur'ān*, ed. Jane Dammen McAuliffe (E. J. Brill, 2021).

35. al-Razi, *al-Tafsir al-kabir*, 11:209.

"I wish I weren't anything." Rather than being burdened with the power and responsibility of governorship, 'Umar wished he was nothing. The companion Bilal, who was a former slave and caller to prayer, would also exclaim, "I wish Bilal's mother did not give birth to him." The statements suggest that if the trial was so significant and painful, then the righteous would sometimes wish they were dead rather than go through the specific ordeal.[36] By comparing Maryam to righteous men such as companions and caliphs, the various exegetical statements demonstrate that the commentators placed Maryam within a Muslim and Islamic history of trial and tribulation. It also reveals that they did not condemn her for wishing for death but rather saw it as a natural part of pain and suffering.[37]

However, in this moment of despair, a voice appears below her, exclaiming, "Do not worry: your lord has provided a stream at your feet and, if you shake the trunk of the palm tree towards you, it will deliver fresh ripe dates for you."[38] The commentators have debated who this voice belongs to: Was it the messenger who appeared earlier on, or was it the baby 'Isa speaking? While both could be possible, what is essential is that the voice guides Maryam on how to act and seek comfort in difficult situations. It commands Maryam to act in "shaking the palm tree" rather than be passive and allow the pain to overtake her. Once she does, she can "eat, drink, be glad" and find comfort in the fruits and stream. The Arabic phrase *be glad* or *be comforted* (*qarri ayna*) is significant here

36. Similarly, Ibn Kathir notes that the statement is permission "to wish for death during a trial." Another statement attributed to the Prophet Muhammad in the end of times is "There will come a time where a man passes by a grave of a man and will say 'I wish I was in his place.'" People would rather be buried in graves than live their lives.

37. Maria Dakake in *The Study Qur'an* states that "Mary's wish to have 'died before this' means that she wished she could have died before the onset of the difficulties she now faced as a woman giving birth to a child alone, without a husband, including both the physical pain of labor and embarrassment about what people would think of her" (Dakake, *The Study Qur'an*, 770).

38. For more on this statement and the role of gender in the narrative, see Kecia Ali, "Destabilizing Gender, Reproducing Maternity: Mary in the Qur'ān," *Journal of the International Qur'anic Studies Association* 2 (2017): 89–109.

because it connects Maryam to another Qur'anic mother, the mother of Musa. After she places Musa in the Nile, the mother worries about her child's safety to the point that she sends her daughter to follow him. When the palace's guards pick up Musa and he does not suckle with any of the women, the daughter shares that she knows a mother who can perform the task. The Qur'an then emphatically states, "We restored him to his mother in this way, so that she might be comforted (*qarra 'aynaha*), not grieve, and know that God's promise is true, though most of them do not know" (28:13). Thus, two Qur'anic mothers—those of Musa and 'Isa—are comforted by God in the early years of motherhood and the birth of their children.

After giving birth, Maryam must now face her people and the fear she had expressed earlier in the story of having a child outside of wedlock. The divine voice tells her "to abstain from conversation" in a similar way to Zakariyya, making it impossible for her to defend herself verbally. When her people see her, they cry out, "Maryam! You have done something terrible! Sister of Aaron! Your father was not an evil man; your mother was not unchaste." Here, they express surprise at how Maryam could have had a child out of wedlock, especially because she comes from a righteous family of chastity and virtue. Instead of responding to their accusations, Maryam affirms her vow of silence and points to her child. The people are astounded and ask incredulously, "How can we converse with an infant?" However, the baby 'Isa miraculously starts to speak, declaring, "I am a servant of God. He has granted me the Scripture; made me a prophet; made me blessed wherever I may be. He commanded me to pray, to give alms as long as I live, to cherish my mother. He did not make me domineering or graceless. Peace was on me the day I was born and will be on me the day I die and the day I am raised to life again." Essential to this monologue is that 'Isa is a human prophet and is commanded to pray and give alms, like other prophets and Muslims. However, it is unique that he is commanded "to cherish his mother" (*barr bi-walidati*), who gave birth to him and was a righteous individual herself. The statement is similar to Yahya, who is noted earlier in the chapter as somebody who was "kind to his parents" (*barr bi-walidayhi*). The section ends with the statement "Such was Jesus, son of Maryam," again emphasizing his human status and relationship to his mother, Maryam.

## Chapter of Maryam: Providing Comfort, Revealing Secrets, and Emphasizing Speech

Along with the narrative of Maryam, the chapter of Maryam (19) comforted Muhammad and the nascent Muslim community, as it is marked with its emphasis on God's favor and mercy. The chapter is understood to have been revealed in the second half of the Meccan period, when "the Meccan disbeliever's contemptuous and oppressive treatment of the Muslims was growing and the Prophet and his followers were faced by the threat of torture and death at their hands."[39] The chapter repeatedly uses the words *your lord* and *mercy* to emphasize the righteous weakness and vulnerability.[40] For instance, when the angel first approaches Maryam, she seeks refuge in God, or "the Most Merciful." The angel will eventually inform Maryam of the birth of 'Isa, stressing that he will be a mercy to all: "We shall make him a sign to all people, a mercy from Us (*rahmatan minna*)." Later in the chapter, Ibrahim pleads with his idolatrous father, explaining that "Satan has rebelled against the Lord of Mercy" and that he fears for him "the punishment from the Lord of Mercy." In his debate with his father, Ibrahim refers to God as "the Most Merciful" (al-Rahman) and tries to win him over with God's mercy. Speaking about the offspring of Adam, Noah, and Abraham and the children of Israel, the chapter declares that "when the revelations of the

39. M. A. S. Abdul Haleem, "Chapter Maryam (19): Providing Muhammad with Comfort," *Journal of Qur'anic Studies* 22, no. 2 (2020): 62.

40. As Leyla Ozgur Alhassen notes regarding the constant repetition of *rahma* and its root of *ra-ha-ma*, "Included in these derivations from the verbal root is also a word that indicates 'womb', 'relationship', and 'kinship' (rahim). Thus, the root ra-ha-ma conveys the concept of mercy and family simultaneously and it adds depth to our understanding of and focus on family in the story." Leyla Ozgur Alhassen, "A Structural Analysis of Surat Maryam, Verses 1–58," *Journal of Qur'anic Studies* 18, no. 1 (2016): 97.

Lord of Mercy were recited to them, they fell to their knees and wept" (19:58). God's mercy is part of the reason why the believers bow down and prostrate. Soon afterward, the Qur'an states that the believers "will enter the Gardens of Lasting Bliss, promised by the Lord of Mercy to His servants" (19:61). Part of God's mercy is guaranteeing paradise to those who believe and do good deeds.

The theme of the Merciful granting the believers paradise is once again emphasized in one of the concluding verses, which states that the "Lord of Mercy" will give love to those who believe and do righteous deeds (19:96). While the word *love* (*hubb*) is used throughout the Qur'an, the specific word used here for *love* (*wudda*) is only referenced this once in the Qur'an and is related to one of the Islamic names of God, al-Wadud, or the Most Loving.[41] Thus, the themes of lordship, mercy, and love run through the entire chapter, from the beginning, which speaks about Maryam, to the middle, which discusses the various prophets, and then the end, which addresses the believers.[42]

The chapter further has a unique rhyme scheme of *ayya*, which runs throughout and is not repeated in other parts of the Qur'an.[43] The rhyme scheme connects the first part of the chapter, which mentions Zakariyya, Maryam, Ibrahim, and other prophets, with the second part, which is a polemic against the disbelievers and a promise of glad tidings to the believers. Thus, the chapter has a distinct coherence that has become

41. Haleem, "Chapter Maryam," 79. Haleem argues, "All this is further evidence to confirm that this sura is a response (*radd*) to the situation and the psychological state of a prophet who was in need of reminders of God's grace and encouragement, such as were given to all previous prophets, and who hoped for similar favour for himself" (80). He also notes, "The repetition of the verbs habli ('grant me') and wahabna ('we granted') must have comforted the Prophet and still, when recited by the most dramatic reciters, on radio and television, and in mosques, in the rhythmic and musical sounds of Qur'anic style, gives hope to those who listen to or read this sura that they too may have their prayers answered from the boundless grace of God" (81).

42. This, of course, does not mean the chapter has polemical verses against the disbelievers. See below.

43. Shawkat Toorawa, "Surat Maryam (Q. 19): Lexicon, Lexical Echoes, English Translation," *Journal of Qur'anic Studies* 13, no. 1 (2011): 25–78.

of increasing interest to modern scholars since the rhyme scheme ties Maryam to other parts of the chapter and other figures and stories.[44] For instance, in verse 19:18, Maryam seeks refuge from the Spirit and asks for him to stay away if he is "pious" (*taqiyya*). This rhyme word of *pious* (*taqiyya*) is used to describe Zakariyya, who is labeled earlier as being pious (*taqiyya*). Later in the chapter (19:63), the Qur'an states that the pious (*taqiyya*) servants will inherit paradise. Thus, the repeated rhyme word *pious* (*taqiyya*) connects Zakariyya, Maryam, and inhabitants of paradise. Similarly, the baby 'Isa states that God "made me devoted to my mother, not one to act overbearing, or with despondency (*shaqiyya*)" (19:32). This same word *despondency* (*shaqiyya*) is used by Zakariyya earlier when he states, "My Lord, my bones have weakened and my head blazes grey, but never in petitioning You, my Lord, have I felt *despondency* (*shaqiyya*)." Zakariyya cries out in a state of weakness and old age, asking for a child and in hope of God. Toward the middle of the chapter, Ibrahim uses the same word after removing himself from his polytheistic father and then turning to God, stating, "I shall pray to my Lord. May I, in petitioning my Lord, not feel despondency (*shaqiyya*)" (19:48). Thus, the words *despondency* and *hopelessness* connect four of the major figures of the chapter: Zakariyya, Maryam, 'Isa, and Ibrahim. These rhyme words act as an "echo" connecting later parts of the chapter with earlier ones and linking certain figures and themes.[45]

---

44. Bilal Gökkir, "Form and Structure of Sura Maryam—A Study from Unity of Sura Perspective," *Süleyman Demirel Üniversitesi İlahiyat Fakültesi Dergisi* 16, no. 1 (2006): 1–16. In his article, Gökkir makes the point that the argument of the coherence of sura Maryam is connected to the larger argument of the coherence of the Qur'an. See also Leyla Ozgur Alhassen, "A Structural Analysis of Sūrat Maryam, Verses 1–58." For discussions of the unit of chapters in the Qur'an in general, see Angelika Neuwirth, *Studien zur Komposition der mekkanischen Suren: Die literarische Form des Koran—ein Zeugnis seiner Historizität? 2., durch eine korangeschichtliche Einführung erweiterte Auflage* (Walter de Gruyter, 2007). Also see Mustansir Mir, "The Sura as a Unity: A Twentieth Century Development in Qur'ān Exegesis," in *Approaches to the Qur'ān*, ed. G. R. Hawting and Abdul-kader A. Shareef (Routledge, 2003), 211–24.

45. For more on Qur'anic allusions and echoes, see Alhassen, *Qur'anic Stories*, 152.

Beyond the rhyme schemes, certain words connect Maryam with other sections and figures in the chapter.[46] For instance, she brings (*ata*) 'Isa to her people, while 'Isa "brings" a book (19:30), and Ibrahim "brings" knowledge to his father (19:43). Even though Maryam is not a "prophet" by most accounts in that she does not come with scripture or divine knowledge, she nonetheless "brings" 'Isa, who is an Islamic prophet and guide.[47] Similarly, Maryam carries (*hamala*) 'Isa in her belly when she is pregnant (19:22) and then once again "carries" him to her people (19:27). The same word, *carry*, is used to discuss how God "carried" the righteous (in the ark) with Noah/Nuh (19:58). Maryam is seen as a vehicle that carries the righteous like the ark, which was divinely inspired and saved. When Maryam is in need and wishes that she were dead and forgotten, a voice "calls out," telling her that she should not be sad (19:24). God provides a stream for her and instructs her to shake the trunk of the palm tree to receive fresh dates so she can "eat, drink, be glad" (19:26). Likewise, Musa is "called out" to prophecy at the burning bush and brought close to God "in a secret communion." Musa is also given support, but this time, it is from his brother Aaron/Harun, who assists his mission and call (19:53).

By looking at the various rhyming words and schemes, a theme of speech and speechlessness emerges throughout the entire chapter. For instance, the chapter begins with the command "to recollect and mention" and then starts with the prayer and petition of Zakariyya. However, to fulfill the prayer, Zakariyya must give up speech and only communicate in signs. Maryam calls out to her lord in her labor pain and wishes she were forgotten. However, when she returns to her people, she is also commanded to be silent, and then it is the baby 'Isa who speaks. Ibrahim asks his father why he worships something that cannot hear, and his progeny is then given a truthful speech (*lisan al-sidq*). Musa is summoned (*nadaynahu*, 19:52), and Israel is described as true to his word (*sadiq al-wa'd*, 19:54). Righteous followers of all the

46. This comparison of words was made possible through the word list Toorawa provides in his article "Surat Maryam," 33–50.

47. The theme of Maryam being a prophet will be discussed in chapter 3.

prophets are described as those who fall down prostrating and weeping when they hear the recitation of the divine word. At the end of the chapter, the Qur'an speaks directly to Muhammad, stating, "We have made it easy through your speech (*lisan*) to bring good tidings to the pious and to warn a stubborn people" (19:98). For Muhammad, the Qur'an's speech comes easily to him and is both a glad tiding and a warning. However, the disbelievers don't have the power of speech, as the last verse notes the destruction of previous peoples and then ends by stating, "Do you perceive anyone of them now, or hear from them the merest murmurs (*rikza*)?" (19:98).

Thus, the theme of speech and speechlessness runs throughout the chapter and is an example of God's omnipotence. In particular to Maryam, she uses her speech first to seek refuge from the visitor and then to question how she will give birth when no man has touched her. When she is alone and during childbirth, she calls out, wishing that she were dead and asking that she were something forgotten. However, when she returns to her people, she is ordered to be silent, and it is God who miraculously makes the infant 'Isa speak. Speech is, therefore, a sign of power and ability, but for the speechless righteous, God provides speech and defense.

When we look at the structural analysis, we also see that the theme of secrets, both revealed and hidden, appears within the chapter.[48] Concerning Maryam, the reader is privy to her intimate conversations and thoughts. We hear, for instance, Maryam's dialogue where she asks for refugee from the angel who appears as a man and her questioning on how she could give birth to a child when she has not had any sexual relations. When she is giving birth, we hear her cry that she wishes she had died and been a thing forgotten.[49] We further hear how she is instructed to shake the palm tree for nourishment and is given a stream to "eat and drink, and put [her] heart at ease." However, there

---

48. Alhassen, "A Structural Analysis of Sūrat Maryam, Verses 1–58," 109.

49. For instance, Sayyid Qutub comments that in this verse, "we almost see her [facial] features, feel the turmoil in her thoughts, and sense the moment of paint that she is in." Sayyid Qutb, *Fi zilal al-Qur'an*, 6 vols (Dar al-Sharuq, 2003), 4:2307.

are ambiguous elements in the narrative that raise the reader's level of interest and curiosity. For instance, we are not explicitly told who the "messenger" is that comes to Maryam or where she removes herself to give birth. We do not know the exact identity of the voice that instructs Maryam to act in her moment of difficulty or the names of the people she appears before when she returns to the town. This play between revealed secrets and ambiguities engages the reader, making them feel close to Maryam, where they hear her inner thoughts and struggles. Yet it also makes the reader feel a sense of mystery and suspense, as they do not fully know the people or contexts of the story.[50] Such a sentiment is captured in the words of the Qur'anic Jesus, who tells God, "You know all that is within me, though I do not know what is within You, You alone have full knowledge of things unseen" (5:118).[51]

## Conclusion

The Qur'an presents Maryam as an independent figure with her own genealogy and miracles, specifically her birth, labor, and inner thoughts and prayers. When the pangs of childbirth begin, she wishes she were dead and forgotten, leading a voice to comfort her. She is commanded not to speak, and when she returns to her people, it is the baby 'Isa who speaks up, defining himself and defending his mother. The chapter of Maryam further provides a distinct coherence regarding rhyme scheme, structure, and theme. The chapter emphasizes God as "the Merciful," engages righteous figures' despair, and provides relief to the believers. The various figures are connected through the idea of speech and silence, and mystery and secrets are found throughout the chapter. Examining Maryam in the Qur'an thus allows us to better understand how Islam views God, righteousness, comfort, and despair.

---

50. Moreover, Alhassen notes that the various Qur'anic stories in the chapter progressively become shorter and increasingly focus on faith and God (Alhassen, "A Structural Analysis of Sūrat Maryam, Verses 1–58," 101).

51. For more on Qur'anic secrets and ambiguities and the idea of the omnipotent and omniscient divine narrator, see Alhassen, *Qur'anic Stories*.

CHAPTER TWO

# Maryam in the Prophetic Literature

WHILE MUCH ATTENTION has been paid to Maryam in the Qur'an, she also plays an important role in prophetic literature, especially reports from the Prophet (*hadith*) and his biography (*sira*). Islam is defined not only by Qur'anic verses but also by the legacy of the Prophet Muhammad and the subsequent Islamic tradition of law, theology, mysticism, art, and dialogue.[1] This normative legacy of the Prophet "is known as the Sunna, and, although it stands second to the Quran in terms of reverence, it is the lens through which the holy book is interpreted and understood."[2] The *Sunna* of the Prophet Muhammad is primarily known through hadith or "reports describing the words, actions, or habits of the Prophet."[3] The hadith are used in law and theology but also in lessons related to character (*akhlaq*) and spirituality. The hadith literature is supplemented by biographical literature, the *sira*, which discusses the life and story of the Prophet Muhammad. While there is an overlap between the hadith and *sira*, the former are shorter and often pithy statements by the Prophet Muhammad, while the latter is his biography.[4]

1. As Jonathan A. C. Brown explains, "Among Western readership, the question 'What does Islam say about' some issue is usually followed by reference to the Quran . . . Yet the Quran is not the [only] source to which a curious reader should refer in order to answer the question 'What does Islam say about' a particular issue." Jonathan A. C. Brown, *Hadith: Muhammad's Legacy in the Medieval and Modern World* (Oneworld, 2009), 3.

2. Brown, *Hadith*, 3.

3. Brown, *Hadith*, 3.

4. Jonathan Brown defines *sira* as "literally 'biography,' generally referring to the biography of the Prophet. *Sīra* is distinct from hadith collections because it follows

In both the hadith and *sira*, Maryam is portrayed as a model of inspiration, ecumenical relations, and communal solidarity. This literature sheds light on how the Qur'anic Mary influenced the lives of the early Muslim community and was a model and spiritual reference to Muhammad.

## Maryam in the Biography of Muhammad (*Sira*)

It is recorded in the early *sira* texts[5] that after Muhammad saw his companions being tortured and persecuted in Mecca, he told them to travel to Abyssinia (*Habasha*).[6] Specifically, he said, "If you travel to the land of Abyssinia, verily in it is a king who does not do injustice to anyone. It is a land of truth until God gives you relief (*faraj*) from what you are in."[7] The famous biographer of the Prophet Muhammad,

a chronological or narrative structure and often includes material without complete *isnads*." Brown, *Hadith*, 289.

5. I draw primarily here from the biography of Muhammad compiled by Ibn Hisham; Montgomery Watt, "Ibn Hisham," in *Encyclopaedia of Islam, Second Edition*, ed. P. Bearman, Th. Bianquis, C. E. Bosworth, E. van Donzel, and W. P. Heinrichs (E. J. Brill, 2021).

6. The chapter on the migration to Abyssinia comes directly after the chapter that details the persecution of the Muslims in Mecca. In particular, it describes how they were physically tortured by putting stones on them and starving them of food and drink. One of the companions, 'Abd Allah b. 'Abbas, notes that the torture was at times so intense that they were not able to sit upright and would even occasionally renounce their faith and affirm the idols of the Meccans. Ibn Hisham, *al-Sira al-Nabawiyya*, ed. 'Umar 'Abd al-Salam Tadmuri, 4 vols. (Dar al-Kitab al-'Arabi, 1999), 1:347.

7. As Wim Raven notes, "We need not doubt that some early Muslims emigrated to Abyssinia nor that commercial relations between Abyssinia and the Arabian Peninsula existed at the time of the Prophet." Wim Raven, "Some Early Islamic Texts on the Negus of Abyssinia," *Journal of Semitic Studies* 33, no. 2 (1988): 197. Sean Anthony translates a letter from 'Urwah Ibn al-Zubayr (d. 93–94/711–13) that attests to the Muslim migration to Abyssinia based on the Mecca persecution: "When that befell the Muslims, the messenger of God commanded them to depart for the land of Abyssinia. In Abyssinia, there was a righteous king called the Negus. None were oppressed in his land, and because of that, word of his righteousness spread.

Ibn Hisham (d. 218/833), then adds, "So the Companions of the Prophet Muhammad left to Abyssinia, fearing tribulation and torture (*fitna*), fleeing towards God with their religion—and this was the first migration (*hijra*) in Islam." Here Ibn Hisham emphasizes how the companions were finding safety in the (Christian) king of Abyssinia, escaping the persecution of the Meccans and engaging in the first migration, one that would foreshadow the famous migration to Medina. This first migration thus helped preserve the religion of Islam and set the foundations of the future Muslim polity in Medina. This migration was further significant as it contained approximately eighty-three companions;[8] notable among them was the Prophet Muhammad's daughter Ruqayya and her husband (and thus the Prophet's son-in-law), the third caliph, 'Uthman ibn Affan.[9] By sending his own daughter, the Prophet Muhammad demonstrated how comfortable he felt sending the early Muslims to Abyssinia and how he believed it was a safe refuge for them. This feeling is echoed by some of the traditions ascribed to the companions who traveled to Abyssinia, such as Umm Salama, who would eventually become one of the wives of the Prophet Muhammad and one

---

The land of Abyssinia was a destination for trade where the Quraysh would conduct business and where they had found a lucrative livelihood, safety, and a fair market, so the Messenger of God commanded them to go there. Most of them went there when they found themselves beleaguered in Mecca. He feared what the trails of persecution [*al-fitan*] would do to them, but he himself remained and did not leave. That remained the case for several years as the Quraysh continued to deal harshly with those who became Muslim. Islam still spread in Mecca after that, and even men from their nobles and indomitable warriors joined the religion." Sean Anthony, *Muhammad and the Empires of Faith: The Making of the Prophet of Islam* (University of California Press, 2020), 111.

8. Ibn Hisham 1:357. Ibn Hisham explains that this number did not include children who traveled with them or were born in Abyssinia.

9. Ibn Hisham 1:349. Iman 'Abbas 'Idan, "Hijra al-Muslimin ila al-Habasha al-Musabbibat wa'l-Nata'ij," *Journal of the Islamic World* 23 (2019): 44–64. See the article for a detailed list of those who migrated to Abyssinia and the various reasons for the migration.

of the "mothers of the believers."[10] As she narrates, "When we descended on the land of Abyssinia, we became the neighbor of the best of neighbors Negus.[11] We were protected in our religion, we worshiped God the most high, we were not harmed and we did not hear anything we did not like."[12] Here Umm Salama contrasts the good treatment she experienced in Abyssinia with the Meccans who persecuted and tortured them.

She continues to relate that when the Meccans heard about the good treatment and safety that the Muslims experienced in Abyssinia, they sent two of their strongest and noblest men, one of whom was the famous politician and diplomat 'Amr b. al-'As.[13] Leatherwork was

---

10. As Ruth Roded explains, "Umm Salama was second only to 'A'isha [*q.v.*] among the female sources of *hadith*; she transmitted over 300, a handful of which are from her alone. Classical Muslim scholars counted her among the legists (*fukaha'*) of the female Companions, a woman of intelligence and sound judgement. She was the last of the Prophet's wives to die, in 59/679, 60/680 or after the massacre of Karbala' [*q.v.*], according to various authorities." Ruth Roded, "Umm Salama Hind," in *Encyclopaedia of Islam*, 2nd ed., ed. P. Bearman, Th. Bianquis, C. E. Bosworth, E. van Donzel, and W. P. Heinrichs (E. J. Brill, 2021).

11. For a discussion of the various traditions surrounding the Negus, see Wim Raven, "Some Early Islamic Texts on the Negus of Abyssinia." For more on Negus, see E. van Donzel, "al-Nadjāshī," in *Encyclopaedia of Islam*, 2nd ed., ed. P. Bearman, Th. Bianquis, C. E. Bosworth, E. van Donzel, and W. P. Heinrichs (E. J. Brill, 2021). For more on Christianity in the biography of the Prophet Muhammad, see Suleiman A. Mourad, "Christians and Christianity in the Sīra of Muḥammad," in *Christian-Muslim Relations 600–1500*, ed. David Thomas (E. J. Brill, 2021). Interestingly, this particular narration of Umm Salama does not correspond with larger tropes that Mourad identifies, such as the fact that Muhammad is foretold in previous scriptures that Islam will eventually vanquish and that Islam condemns Christianity. Nonetheless, the narration does speak to the idea of a story "employed to validate Muhammad's claim to be a prophet and legitimize Islam as a religious tradition following on after Christianity."

12. Ibn Hisham 1:360.

13. As A. J. Wensick notes, 'Amr "passed for one of the most wily politicians of his time, and we must endorse this verdict." 'Amr would go on to convert to Islam and play major roles in the battles of succession. He would eventually become the governor of Egypt. A. J. Wensinck, "'Amr b. al-'Āṣ," in *Encyclopaedia of Islam*, 2nd ed., ed. P. Bearman, Th. Bianquis, C. E. Bosworth, E. van Donzel, and W. P. Heinrichs (E. J. Brill; 2021).

greatly prized in Mecca, so they came with the finest leather as gifts to all of the bishops to win them over and have them return the Muslims to them. The Meccans' plan was first to share the gifts with the Negus and his council and then ask for the return of the Muslims. The Meccan messengers initially approached the bishops and then, after giving them their gifts, asked for an opportunity to communicate directly with the Negus. The inner circle agreed, and the Meccan messengers came before the Abyssinian king and explained, "Some foolish young men and women[14] of our people have taken refuge in this kingdom. They have left their own religion, not for yours, but for one they have invented, one that is unknown to us and yourselves. The nobles of their people, who are their fathers, their uncles, and their kinsmen, beg you to restore them to them."[15] The narration suggests that the companions' relatives wanted the Muslims back and felt upset they had abandoned them.

At first, the bishops agreed, saying that both men had spoken the truth and that their people knew best of their affairs and what troubled them. Thus, the king should submit the people to the Meccan messengers so they can be returned to their people and their land. However, the Negus became upset and refused to give up the Muslims without hearing from them first, noting they had chosen him as a source of protection: "No, by God, they shall not be betrayed—a people that have sought my protection and made my country their home and chosen me above all others!"[16] Here the Negus demonstrates his commitment to justice by making sure he hears both sides.

---

14. Here, the Meccan messengers use the word *ghulman*, which could be translated as *children* or *older children who are about to reach puberty*. Using this word could describe the Abyssinian refugees as youths but also mock them and suggest they had no wisdom.

15. Martin Lings, *Muhammad: His Life Based on the Earliest Sources* (Inner Traditions, 2006), 83.

16. This story has been used in the modern discourse of jurisprudence of Muslim minorities (*fiqh al-aqalliyyat*), refugees, and migration. Sami A. Aldeeb Abu-Sahlieh, "The Islamic Conception of Migration," *International Migration Review* 30, no. 1, (1996): 37–57; Zeki Saritoprak, "An Islamic Approach to Migration and Refugees," *CrossCurrents* 67, no. 3 (2017): 522–531; Andrew F. March, "Sources of

The Negus then summoned the Muslims and asked, "What is this religion which has separated you from your people and you have not entered into my religion or any other religious communities?" Ja'far b. Abi Talib,[17] the cousin of the Prophet and an eloquent spokesperson, answered on their behalf:

> Oh King, we were a people steeped in ignorance, worshipping idols, eating unsacrificed carrion, committing abominations, breaking ties of our kin, being ill to the neighbors, and the strong would devour the weak. Thus we were, until God sent us a messenger from out of our midst, one whose lineage we knew, and his veracity, trustworthiness and integrity. He called us unto God, that we should testify to His Oneness and worship Him and repudiate[18] what we and our fathers had worshipped in the way of stones and idols; and he commanded us to speak truly, to fulfill our promises, to respect the ties of kinship and be good to the neighbors, and to refrain from what is forbidden and from bloodshed. He prohibited us from abominations, lying, devouring the money of the orphans, and

---

Moral Obligation to Non-Muslims in the 'Jurisprudence of Muslim Minorities' (Fiqh al-aqalliyyāt) Discourse," *Islamic Law and Society* 16, no. 1 (2009): 34–94; Khaled Abou El Fadl, "Islamic Law and Muslim Minorities: The Juristic Discourse on Muslim Minorities from the Second/Eighth to the Eleventh/Seventeenth Centuries," *Islamic Law and Society* 1, no. 2 (1994): 141–187; Khaled Abou El Fadl, "Legal Debates on Muslim Minorities: Between Rejection and Accommodation," *Journal of Religious Ethics* 22, no. 1 (1994): 127–162. For a thorough discussion of how Abyssinia fits within modern Muslim discourse on the jurisprudence of Muslim minorities, see Uriya Shavit, "Europe, the New Abyssinia: On the Role of the First Hijra in the Fiqh al-Aqalliyyāt al-Muslima Discourse," *Islam and Christian–Muslim Relations* 29, no. 3 (2018): 371–391.

17. Ibn Ishaq narrates a tradition that it was 'Uthman who spoke to the Negus, but the dominant narrations say otherwise.

18. The verb used here is *khala'a*, which literally means to *take off*, such as taking off a garment.

> slandering chaste women.[19] He commanded us to worship God alone, and not associate anything with him, and commanded us to pray, to pay alms and fast[20] . . . We affirmed him, believed in him and followed him on what has come from God. We worship God alone and we do not associate anything with him counting as forbidden what He has forbidden and as licit what He has allowed. For these reasons, our people turned against us, tortured us and persecuted us to make us forsake our religion and return to the worship of idols from the worship of God, and to regard as lawful the evil deeds we once committed. So when they persecuted us, were unjust to us, circumscribed our lives and came in the way between us and our religion, we left to your country and chose you above all others, desiring your hospitality, hoping that with you, oh king, we would not be treated unjustly.[21]

Here we hear from Ja'far the essence of the emerging Islamic faith, such as the beliefs in monotheism, prophecy, and prayer. Yet the Islamic message was not only spiritual but also one that challenged the Meccan status quo, where the "strong would devour the weak" and those on the margins of society were neglected. Their challenge led them to be persecuted and then become refugees to the land of Abyssinia.

On hearing Ja'far's response, the Negus asked, "Do you have anything from what God has given you" or in regard to scripture? Ja'far responded in the affirmative. The Negus then told him "to read it to me," so Ja'far read a portion of the beginning of the chapter of Maryam

19. The word *muhsanat* usually refers to married women.

20. Umm Salama notes here that Ja'far then listed the commandments of the Islamic faith.

21. Ibn Hisham 1:362.

(which is detailed in the previous chapter).[22] Umm Salama records that the Negus wept until his beard became wet, and the inner circle also wept until the scrolls in front of them were soaked. The Negus then reportedly said, "This has truly come from the same source (*al-mishkat al-wahida*)[23] as that which Jesus brought."[24] He turned to the two envoys of the Quraysh tribe and stated, "You may go, for by God I will not deliver them unto you; they shall not be betrayed."[25]

However, the Meccan messengers did not give up, and 'Amr b. al-'As devised another plan to tell the Negus what the Muslims believed about Jesus: "By God, we will tell him that they falsely believe that Jesus the son of Maryam is (simply) a servant!" The next day, they returned to the Negus saying, "Oh king, what they say about Jesus the son of Mary is distressing and terrible (*'azim*)! Send to them and ask them what they say about him." The Negus obliged and sent for the Muslims to ask them about Jesus. Umm Salama interjects that "nothing (this severe) had ever descended upon us (the Muslims)!" The statement demonstrates how tense and dire the situation was for the nascent Muslim community and how they feared being returned to Mecca.

---

22. In Ibn Hisham, the chapter of Maryam is referred to by its opening letters, or *Kaf Ha Ya 'Ayn Sad*, which could suggest that it was not yet known by the name Surat Maryam.

23. Here, the Negus literally states that the scripture comes from the same "lamp," suggesting that both came from the same divine light.

24. The famous scholar Ibn Taymiyya mentions this story and repeatedly emphasizes the phrase "from the same source" in his famous polemic against Christianity. For Ibn Taymiyya, the story affirms the continuous nature of the Islamic revelation and how Muhammad continued the message of Moses and Jesus. He also spends a good deal of time discussing how the Prophet prayed for the Negus after he died and told them to pray for "their brother." Ibn Taymiyya, *al-Jawab al-sahib li-man baddala din al-Masih*, ed. 'Ali b. Hasan b. Nasir, 'Abd al-'Aziz b. Ibrahim 'Askar, and Hamd b. Muhammad Hamdan, 7 vols. (Dar al-'Asima, 1999), 2: 247–263.

25. As Saritoprak notes, "Through his actions, the Negus exemplified the Islamic approach to refugees, one that stresses compassion, mercy, and protection over self-interest." Saritoprak, "An Islamic Approach to Migration and Refugees," 526.

The Muslims met privately and asked each other, "What do you say about Jesus the son of Mary if you were asked about him?" Some responded, "By God, we say what God has said and what our prophet has brought, come what may." When they were brought to the Negus once again, Ja'far responded to his question, "We say what our prophet has said: He [Jesus] is the servant of God, his messenger, spirit and word who was put (*alqa*) into Mary the blessed virgin." Umm Salama then narrates that the Negus hit the earth with his hand, picked up a stick, and declared, "By God, what differentiates between us and Jesus the Son of Mary is this stick." In response, the bishops gasped and snorted, disapproving of the Negus's declaration. Nonetheless, the Negus disregarded their reactions and instructed the Muslims, "Go, you are safe in this land." The Negus then commanded that the gifts be returned to the Meccan emissaries, as he had no need for them and did not want to take a bribe. The Meccan emissaries finally left dejected and disgraced, as their plan to bring back the Muslims had failed.[26] The Muslims celebrated their victory and later prayed for the Negus to vanquish his enemies and continue to rule throughout the land.[27]

---

26. It was also recorded that the Negus said he would not hurt the companions even if he were offered a mountain of gold. Mourad cites a variant tradition, "which narrates the circumstances of the conversion of the famous 'Amr ibn al-'As to Islam; it is said that 'Amr, who was the Meccan envoy, asked the Negus to hand over the leader of the Muslim immigrants so that he could kill him. The Negus struck 'Amr on the nose, causing it to bleed, and said angrily, 'Do you have no shame! You dare ask me to hand over to you the envoy of the messenger of God who is visited by the angel Gabriel (*al-namus al-akbar*), who used to come to Moses and Jesus son of Mary!' 'Amr asked the Negus about the truthfulness of Muhammad's religious claims and the Abyssinian ruler affirmed that it was the truth and that soon Muhammad would have dominion over those who opposed him."

27. Umm Salama then records that the Negus faced internal opposition from a member of his kingdom, leading the Muslims to pray for his victory over his enemy and to regain control over the land (Ibn Hisham 1:366). The belief that the Negus became Muslim but hid his belief set a precedent for *taqiyya*, or hiding one's true beliefs for one's safety (Raven, "Some Early Islamic Texts on the Negus of Abyssinia," 204). Raven further suggests that the funeral prayer for the Negus was a way to contrast his actions with those of the Hypocrites in Medina: "Perhaps that the Negus, though officially not a Muslim, deserved on account of his noble deeds funeral prayers

The story demonstrates from an early time how Mary became a bridge and interfaith figure for the nascent Muslim community. When the Muslims were summoned and asked to recite from scripture, Ja'far chose to read from the chapter of Maryam, which details her story about how she became pregnant and gave birth to Jesus. The verses reportedly had a profound effect on the Negus and his inner circle to the point that Umm Salama records that he and the bishops wept after hearing the recitation. Their tears represented an affinity with the Islamic depiction of Mary, which details her spiritual, physical, and emotional struggles.

However, the episode also demonstrates how Jesus could function as a divisive figure between Christians and Muslims. When the Meccan messengers were first sent away, they devised a plan to question the Muslims about Jesus, as they understood that Islamic beliefs regarding him did not correspond with Christian ones. This created anxiety and fear among the Muslims, who knew their belief that Jesus was only a servant and messenger of God might not go over well with the Negus and the bishops and could subsequently jeopardize their residence in Abyssinia. Thus, interfaith encounters, even early ones such as this, are often tied to politics, as there are tangible resources, rewards, and incentives at stake.

The story further suggests that the Muslim view of Mary and Jesus (and Christianity as a whole) was already forming in the middle and late Meccan period. While Muslims increasingly encountered Christians later in Medina, their theology regarding monotheism and prophecy was already taking shape in the early era. This theology was known not only to the Muslims but also to their Meccan detractors, who knew that the Muslims did not believe that Jesus was the son of God. However, their message was still new, as the Negus and bishops were unaware of it and thus had to ask several questions to better understand their beliefs. The Islamic religion was still nascent and did not fit within the existing religious communities in the Near East. The Meccan detractors even

---

more than many a pseudo-Muslim" (Raven, "Some Early Islamic Texts on the Negus of Abyssinia," 210).

describe Islam as an "innovated" (*mubtada'*) religion that was unknown to the Arabs, the Negus, and the bishops.[28]

Last, we hear about this interfaith encounter through the words of Umm Salama, a woman and future wife of the Prophet. Her narrative is full of detail, suspense, drama, and emotion. At times, she pauses her narration and exclaims how she and the refugee Muslim community felt and how the entire situation affected their mental and emotional state. For instance, when the Meccans returned to question the Muslims about Jesus, she exclaimed that "nothing (this severe) had ever descended upon us!" Her narration details the struggles, trials, and beliefs of the early Muslim community, where they articulate their creed while fearing retribution. She feels a deep bond with the Muslims and identifies with them, knowing that her personal safety and well-being were interconnected with the others'. Thus, the story of the Islamic Mary is not simply carried on by men but by other women who identify with her and her spiritual struggles.

## Maryam in the Conquest of Mecca

While Maryam appears in the beginning of the *sira*, she also appears toward the end. When the Muslims finally returned victorious to Mecca, Muhammad ordered that the Ka'ba be cleansed of all the idols and icons, representing a new beginning of the worship of one God. However, several traditions record that the interior of the Ka'ba held

28. Moreover, the story reveals the Arab and Muslim connection to Africa. The Muslims did not initially migrate to an Arab polity but rather an African one, which had a different culture, language, and religion than their own. They appear to speak in translation but were nonetheless able to communicate their concerns and beliefs clearly and in a way that was understood by their hosts. The Arabs and Meccans had a previous relationship with Abyssinia and an idea of which gifts they would appreciate and welcome. They speak to Negus as a colleague and ally, but their request is ultimately rejected, as Negus felt an affinity toward the beliefs of the Muslim community and was sympathetic to their status as a persecuted minority community. Arabia was thus not the isolated backwater that is often depicted in popular culture and movies.

depictions of Maryam that Muhammad hesitated to erase.[29] In one tradition, Muhammad found that the Kaʿba had pictures of angels and the patriarch Ibrahim and his son Ismaʿil casting lots with arrows. He then saw a picture of Maryam, put his hand on it, and declared, "Erase all the depictions in [the Kaʿba] except the picture of Maryam."

The tradition suggests that the Prophet Muhammad had a unique connection with Maryam, as he put his hand on her image and was ready to erase all of them except hers. While some narrations suggest there were separate icons of Maryam and Jesus, others state that the depictions had the baby Jesus sitting in Maryam's lap (*fi hijriha*).[30] These ancillary traditions add Jesus as one of the icons Muhammad refused to erase. These various traditions speak to the fact that there were pictures of both Jesus and Maryam in the Kaʿba and that Muhammad ordered all of them to be removed except an image of the two.[31]

The art thus connects the Kaʿba to a larger network of religious shrines and places of worship, many of which were Christian.[32] The Kaʿba not only housed Arab idols but also revered biblical figures of

29. G. R. D. King, "The Paintings of the Pre-Islamic Kaʿba," *Muqarnas* 21 (2004): 219–229. See also K. A. C. Creswell, "The Kaʿba in A.D. 608," *Archaeologia: or Miscellaneous Tracts Relating to Antiquity* 94 (1951): 97–102.

30. King, "The Paintings of the Pre-Islamic Kaʿba," 221.

31. King, "The Paintings of the Pre-Islamic Kaʿba," 220. King shares one tradition to this effect: "Sulayman [b. Musa al-Shami] said to ['Ata' b. Abi Rabah], 'The pictures of the representations (*tamathil suwar*) of devils ('afarit, sc. *idols*) that were in the House [i.e., the Kaʿba], who obliterated them?' He said: 'I do not know, other than that they were obliterated, with the exception of those two pictures ['Isa b. Maryam and Maryam]. I saw them [i.e., the rest] and their obliteration.' Ibn Jurayj said: 'Then 'Ata' returned to the sketch of the six columns that he had drawn in the plan.' Then he said: 'The representation of 'Isa and his mother, upon them be peace, was in the middle of the row in front of the door that we came through when we entered [the Kaʿba].' My grandfather [Ahmad b. Muhammad al-Azraqi] said: 'Dawud b. 'Abd al-Rahman told me that 'Amr b. Dinar said: "A [picture] of 'Isa b. Maryam and his mother were set in the interior of the Kaʿba before the destruction of the idols."'"

32. Based on a reading of Ibn Hisham, Creswell argues that one of the builders of the Kaʿba in 608 was an Abyssinian Christian. The reconstruction of the Kaʿba is described as using wood, and its architecture resembles churches found in Ethiopia.

Abraham, Jesus, and Maryam. Depictions of Mary and Jesus, especially with Jesus in Mary's lap, would eventually become more widespread, but they were already found in seventh-century Christian art in the region, from Egypt to Palestine. Moreover, as the narration above notes, Mary and Jesus were not the only pictures but were rather included with those of angels, prophets, and righteous figures. Pictures of Mary and Jesus surrounded by saints and apostles existed in Egypt and the surrounding region in the seventh century.[33]

Various medieval and modern scholars found these narrations problematic. Not only do they lack complete chains of transmission and are not part of the mainstream *sira* and hadith tradition, but they also raise the theological problem of the Prophet Muhammad making an exception for icons of Maryam (and Jesus) and speak against the plethora of reports where he erased all the depictions. For instance, in the most authoritative hadith collection of al-Bukhari (d. 256/870), the Prophet Muhammad refused to go into the Ka'ba while the various idols were still inside, so he ordered them removed. Among them was the picture of Ibrahim and Isma'il casting lots. After the pictures were removed, he entered the Ka'ba and said, "God is great" in its various corners.[34] This tradition differs from the ones cited above in that it does not include the addition of the Prophet Muhammad seeing the picture of Maryam (and Jesus). It further suggests that all the idols and pictures were removed before the Prophet entered the space.

However, it could have been that all the icons were ordered to be removed, but those of Jesus and Maryam were originally out of sight, leading Muhammad to discover them later. Another possibility is that Muhammad ordered that all the portable idols be destroyed, leaving the murals to be erased at another time.[35] A third is that Muhammad

The finding once again demonstrates the connection between Arabia and Abyssinia, which is noted in the early biography of the Prophet Muhammad.

33. King, "The Paintings of the Pre-Islamic Ka'ba," 221.

34. King, "The Paintings of the Pre-Islamic Ka'ba," 223.

35. King, "The Paintings of the Pre-Islamic Ka'ba," 220.

initially hesitated to erase the depiction of Maryam but later decided to do so to be consistent in his actions. Even if the traditions are not authentic, they demonstrate the Muslim memory of Muhammad having a special connection with Maryam and deeply identifying with her as a spiritual and religious figure.

## Maryam in Prophetic Reports (Hadith)

The story of Maryam continues from the literature regarding the biography of the Prophet Muhammad to his prophetic reports, or hadith. The various traditions taken together demonstrate that hadith collectors often grouped reports regarding Maryam and mentioned them in chapters dealing with interpreting the Qur'an and providing details on the lives of the prophets. They further demonstrate that the Prophet Muhammad held Maryam in high regard and believed her to be a model of piety and faith that people, especially women, could strive toward.

The hadith collections often explain Qur'anic verses by providing a commentary on reports and presenting the Prophet as an interpreter of the Qur'an. For instance, in his chapter on the prophets, the famous hadith collector al-Bukhari cites several traditions about Maryam, including comments on the Qur'anic description of her as chosen (*istafa*), purified, and selected above all the women of creation (see the previous chapter).[36] Al-Bukhari provides a report narrated by 'Ali, cousin of the Prophet Muhammad and a caliph after him, that states, "The best of women is Maryam bint 'Umran and the best of women is Khadija (the first wife of the Prophet Muhammad)."[37] Here the Prophet Muhammad refers to Maryam as a "daughter," which corresponds to how the Qur'an often describes her.[38] He further connects Maryam with

36. Al-Bukhari, *Sahih al-Bukhari* (Dar Ibn Kathir, 2002), 850.

37. Al-Bukhari, *Sahih al-Bukhari*, 850. This tradition is also cited in other hadith collections in a chapter of the companions on the Prophet Muhammad since it mentions Khadija.

38. See the previous chapter for Maryam's Qur'anic portrayal. As Salem states, "Based on this context of Qur'ānic references to the same women in the 'four women of

Khadija, his first wife and confidant. Despite their radically different times and places, the Prophet Muhammad extols both for their piety and faith.

Commentators understand this hadith to refer to the fact that Maryam and Khadija were the best women of their times, as similar phrases are used to describe them. An alternative reading would be that Maryam and Khadija were both the best women of all time, which is similar to other traditions that discuss their statuses. Hadith commentators further raise the question of whether Maryam was a prophet, especially since the word *chosen* is used (*istafa*) and she is mentioned alongside other prophets in the Qur'anic chapter of Maryam.[39] Moreover, there is no contradiction between her being sincere and trustworthy (*siddiqa*) and her being a prophet (*nabiyya*) since other prophets, like Joseph/Yusuf, were understood to be both. Nonetheless, others disagree, believing that Maryam was not a prophet since no explicit Qur'anic verse or hadith said she was.[40]

Immediately after this hadith, al-Bukhari cites a tradition where the Prophet Muhammad extols the status of his wife 'Ayisha among women and states, "Many men have become 'complete' (*kamala*) but the only one who has become 'complete' among the women is Maryam the daughter of 'Umran and 'Asiya the wife of Pharaoh."[41] Here the Prophet

Paradise *hadith*,' it can be argued that the femaleness of the four characters is not intended to delimit the extent of their piety as distinctively inferior to that of male counterparts, but rather to highlight the extent to which women can attain piety that can exceed that of men while also being independent of them." Feryal Salem, "Women in the *Hadith* Literature," in *The Oxford Handbook of Islam and Women*, ed. Asma Afsaruddin (Oxford University Press, 2023), 69.

39. Ibn Hajar al-Asqalani, *Fath al-bari bi-sharh al-Bukhari*, ed. Muhammad Fu'ad 'Abd al-Baqi, and Muhibb al-Din al-Katib (al-Maktaba al-Salafiyya, 1911), 6: 470. For more on hadith commentary, see Joel Blecher, *Said the Prophet of God: Hadith Commentary Across a Millennium* (University of California Press, 2017); Joel Blecher and Stefanie Brinkmann, eds., *Hadith Commentary: Continuity and Change* (Edinburgh University Press, 2023).

40. This topic of Maryam being a prophet will be discussed in the next chapter.

41. Al-Bukhari, *Sahih al-Bukhari*, 850.

Muhammad connects his wife ʿAyisha with Maryam, whom he refers to as a "daughter," which is similar to the tradition cited before. There is a further connection with Asiya, the wife of Pharaoh, who is mentioned in the Qur'an as the one who finds Musa in the Nile and saves him from Pharaoh's wrath and possible attempt at murder. The tradition thus has an "Abrahamic" underpinning, as it links women from the time of Islam, Christianity, and Judaism. The tradition is also reminiscent of the end of chapter 66:11–12, which puts forward Asiya and Maryam as models for all believers, including the wives of the Prophet Muhammad, because of their devoutness and opposition to injustice. It further distinguishes Maryam among women as the only one who has become "whole" and one of the best of all time, which corresponds to the Qur'an (3:43).

A final tradition in this chapter of al-Bukhari speaks about Maryam in relation to the women of Quraysh, who were considered to be the best Arabian tribe, as they were the custodians of the Kaʿba and were the tribe of the Prophet Muhammad himself. The Prophet states that the women of Quraysh were the "best of women," highlighting that they ride on camels, are kind to their children, and are strong caretakers of their spouses. This tradition initially appears to be in contradiction with the traditions before since it suggests that the women of the Quraysh were the best, not Maryam or other non-Arabs. Nonetheless, the narrator of the tradition, the companion Abu Hurayra, notes after the report that "Maryam the daughter of ʿImran never rode a camel." The clarification suggests that even though Maryam was not from the Quraysh tribe and did not do honorable things (such as riding camels), she was still considered among the best women based on the traditions cited above. The addition is significant because it asserts that a non-Arabs, such as Maryam, could still be considered superior because of their piety and faith.[42]

42. Jacqueline Hoover cites this tradition as an example that "in Islam [Maryam] is eclipsed by the Muslim women of the early Islamic community who fit the Islamic model of womanhood to a greater degree." However, I believe the tradition and its place within the hadith collection suggest that Maryam was still honorable despite

In some lesser-known collections, several traditions speak to the superiority of Maryam as well as those women in the time of Musa and the Prophet Muhammad.[43] For instance, one tradition states, "The best women of all of creation are four: Mary the daughter of ʿImran, Asiya the daughter of Muzahim the wife of Pharaoh, Khadija the daughter of Khuwaylid (the wife of Muhammad), and Fatima the daughter of Muhammad."[44] The tradition references all of the women as "daughters" and adds to the list Fatima, the daughter of Khadija and the Prophet Muhammad. Based on this tradition, some scholars held Maryam to be the greatest of all women since she is mentioned first. The list also encompasses different types of women, from Maryam, a single mother, and Asiya, a foster mother (to Musa), to Khadija, a wife (of the Prophet Muhammad) and Fatima, a daughter (of the Prophet Muhammad). The list, therefore, encompasses the different roles and archetypes that women play in their various families and communities, from daughters to wives to mothers.

A second set of traditions discusses the women in relation to paradise: "The best women of Paradise are Khadija the daughter of Khuwaylid, Fatima the daughter of Muhammad, Mary the daughter of ʿImran, and Asiya the daughter of Muzahim the wife of Pharaoh." A similar narration states, "The mistresses of the women of Paradise after Mary are Fatima and Khadija." These traditions suggest that Maryam was not only the best woman of all time but also a leader in paradise and

---

her not being from the Quraysh tribe. The tradition implies that even though Maryam "did not ride camels," she continues to be a model of emulation. As Hoover later explains, the tradition "does point out that Maryam lived in a different time and place." Jacqueline Hoover, "Mary/Maryam as a Prophet in the Islamic and Christian Traditions," in *Prophets in the Qur'ān and the Bible*, ed. Sin-jong Paek and Sam Kim (Wipf and Stock, 2022), 181.

43. See Younus Y. Mirza, "Islamic Mary: Between Prophecy and Orthodoxy," *Journal of Qur'anic Studies* 23, no. 3 (2021): 78–79.

44. Mirza, "Islamic Mary," 78–79.

the hereafter. They further connect the women of Prophet Muhammad's time to that of Musa's and 'Isa's.[45]

A last set of traditions appears in the section devoted to the merits of Fatima but continues to emphasize Maryam's role as the "best woman of all time" and "the mistress of paradise." In these traditions, the Prophet Muhammad calls over Fatima after the day of the Meccan conquest to converse privately with her. He begins to speak, and she cries; then he speaks more, and she laughs. After the Prophet Muhammad died, she was asked, "Why did you cry and why did you laugh?" Fatima explained, "The Prophet Muhammad informed me that he was going to die so I cried. Then he informed me that I was the mistress of the women of paradise except for Maryam the daughter of 'Imran so I laughed."[46] The tradition draws a parallel between Maryam and Fatima in that they are both the mistresses of paradise and daughters of great men who came from pious families. Yet it also implies that Maryam is greater, as Fatima is the mistress of paradise "except for" Maryam. The tradition is therefore consistent with the Qur'anic verse that Maryam is "the best of all time" and even superior to the various women in the life of the Prophet Muhammad. However, as we will see, Shi'i theologians and traditions held that Fatima was the best woman based on her relationship to the Prophet, marriage to 'Ali, and as mother to the Shi'i Imams Hasan and Husayn.

## Conclusion

The prophetic biography (*sira*) and reports (hadith) both demonstrate a deep reverence for Maryam, as her memory plays an important role in the development of the nascent Muslim community. The early Muslim refugees read the chapter of Maryam to the king of Abyssinia as a way

45. The reports also are reminiscent of verses 66:11–12, which indicates that 'Asiya's prayer of entering paradise is answered.

46. Muhammad b. 'Isa al-Tirmidhi, *al-Jami' al-kabir*, ed. Bashshar 'Awwad Ma'ruf, 6 vols. (Dar al-Gharb al-Islami, 1996), 177.

to explain their beliefs and seek safety from the pagan Meccans. The recitation reportedly had a profound effect on the Negus, as he wept and eventually allowed the Muslims to stay within his kingdom. After the conquest of Mecca, various traditions describe the Prophet Muhammad as hesitating to remove pictures of Maryam from the Ka'ba, with some stating that he ordered everything to be erased except for her image, as well as some suggesting her depictions were removed only afterward. The prophetic reports further connect Maryam to the women of the Prophet's time, most notably Khadija and Fatima, demonstrating that she was a model of faith and piety despite her being non-Arab and emerging outside the Arab community.

CHAPTER THREE

# Maryam in Theology

MARYAM ALSO APPEARS in discussions of Islamic theology, or how the Muslim community defined its faith based on the scriptural sources of the Qur'an, Sunna, and Muslim memory. The nascent Muslim community had to explain itself against competing religions and ideologies, showing that it was similar but also distinct from those that surrounded it.[1] The members sought to create a coherent theological structure that could classify different historical figures who would withhold the scrutiny of other Muslims and external distractors and polemicists. Since Maryam played a prominent role within the core scriptures of the Qur'an and prophetic legacy (Sunna), it was essential to find a place for her among the righteous and worthy of emulation.[2] It is here that Maryam appears in the discussion of Islamic theology. But what role did she play in executing God's will? Was she a saint, a friend of God, or a prophet? Moreover, Maryam was a woman, leading scholars to debate her place among other females and whether she could be ranked higher

1. A. J. Wensinck, *The Muslim Creed: Its Genesis and Historical Development* (Cambridge University Press, 1932), 1.

2. Ahmad ibn Muhammad Tahawi, *The Creed of Imam al-Tahawi*, trans. Hamza Hanson Yusuf (Zaytuna Institute, 2007). While Maryam was seen as righteous in the Qur'an and prophetic tradition, Muslims would later have to categorize her within their theologies and in comparison to other figures of emulation. The categorization had to withstand the questioning of other religious traditions as Islam spread and interacted with other belief systems and religions. Specifically, Muslims had to contend with Christian theologians who understood Mary within their own categorization and had competing claims to her status. Thus, the theology of Maryam only crystallized in response to both intra-Muslim and interreligious debates around her status and positionality.

than men. Various theologians devised different hierarchies of where Maryam fit and how she should be understood and categorized.

## The Prophets

To best understand where Maryam fits within the Islamic theological structure, it is helpful to present an overview of the most important theological category: the prophets. Key to Islamic theology was the idea of prophetology, or that God sent prophets and messengers to humanity to guide them to the straight path and to worship God himself. The concept undergirds the claim that the Prophet Muhammad himself was a prophet, a key component of being a Muslim and a follower of Islam.

The idea of God sending guidance from the heavens is captured in early theology texts, which state, "We believe in the angels, the prophets, the revealed books that were sent to the messengers—We testify that they are on a clear truth."[3] The fact that the creed groups the prophets with the angels and sacred books is significant because they are all ways for God to communicate with humanity and agents of his divine actions. In a cosmology where the divine is transcendent and distinct, God does not appear on earth to direct actions and events. However, the angels, prophets, and scripture act on God's behalf and communicate his wishes and moral vision to humanity.

The grouping of angels, scripture, and prophets is presented in several Qur'anic verses. For instance, Qur'an 2:285 states, "The messenger believes in what has been sent down to him from his Lord, as do the faithful. They all believe in God, His angels, His scriptures, and His messengers. 'We make no distinction between any of His messengers,' they say, 'We hear and obey. Grant us Your forgiveness, our Lord. To You we all return!'" The verse brings together the angels, scriptures, and messengers as a means for God to communicate his actions and implement his will. The verse presents the model of a true believer who

3. 'Ali b. 'Ali b. Muhammad b. Abi al-'Izz, *Sharh al-'Aqidah al-Tahawiyya*, ed. 'Abd Allah b. al-Muhsin al-Turki and Shu'ayb al-Arna'ut (Mu'assasat al-Risalah, 1987), 410.

exclaims that they will "hear and obey," ask for forgiveness, and testify that the ultimate end is up to God. Another verse (2:177) states, "Goodness does not consist in turning your face towards East or West. The truly good are those who believe in God and the Last Day, in the angles, the Scripture, and the prophets." Once again, the verse discusses the angels, scripture, and prophets together as a way to communicate to humanity and adds the importance of believing in God and in the hereafter. The verse continues to explain "goodness" as represented by those people who give away their wealth and are good to their relatives, orphans, those in need, travelers, beggars, and slaves. They also pray, give alms, keep their pledges, and are steadfast in the face of misfortune, adversity, and danger. The verse implies that the prophets and scripture command these positive traits and characteristics. To reach true faith and character, one must embrace the idea of prophets and scripture and follow their teachings and commandments.[4]

Moreover, the Qur'an states (4:163) that it has sent revelation to Muhammad, as it has done to those before such as the biblical prophets Nuh, Ibrahim, Ishaq, Isma'il, and Musa. The following verse explains that (4:164) "to other messengers We have already mentioned to you, and also to some We have not." The verses thus affirm the great biblical prophets such as Abraham and Musa but also lesser-known ones whose stories God has not revealed. The verse depicts a picture of a multitude of prophets sent to different people and that they called toward the truth and the divine.[5] The duty of the messengers and prophets was to

4. Abi al-'Izz notes that one does not "truly believe except with following the messengers." Belief in the messengers was a key point of contention between Muslim orthodoxy and the rationalists or philosophers who did not necessarily believe in scripture or messengers to truth. One's rational faculties, they believed, could arrive at the worship of God without intermediaries. Abi al-'Izz, *Sharh al-'Aqidah al-Tahawiyya*, 402.

5. See also 40:78: "We have sent other messengers before you—some We have mentioned to you and some We have not."

proclaim the messenger (*al-balagh al-mubin*), but it was not necessarily their responsibility if their people headed their call.[6]

## The Friend of God—the *Wali*

In addition to the prophets, there was a category of believers who were considered to be a *wali* (plural *awliya'*), which could be defined in a variety of ways from a friend, an ally, and a supporter or even a saint. These believers were different from prophets in the sense that they did not receive direct revelation from God nor were tasked with calling their people to the divine. The term *wali* is connected to the concept of *wilaya*, which connotes *protection* and *support*. Various Qur'anic verses speak about *wilaya* such as verse 10:62, which states, "But for those who are on God's side (*awliya'*) there is no fear, nor shall they grieve." The friends of God are unique because they ultimately do not have to worry about debilitating fear and sadness. The verse continues that those on God's side are "those who believe and are conscious of God" and that they have glad tidings in this life and the hereafter. Commentators connect the verses and see them as a continuation where belief and piety are an extension of *wilaya*.[7] Another verse (2:257) states, "God is the ally (*wali*) of those who believe: He brings them out of the depths of

6. The prophets were then subdivided between those who were prophets, which was the general term, and messengers, which was more specific to a prophet who also came with scripture. The prophets were also divided into the "persevering ones" such as Noah/Nuh, Abraham/Ibrahim, Moses/Musa, Jesus/'Isa, and Muhammad. The Qur'an captures these special prophets in various verses that speak about pledges and covenants: "We took a solemn pledge from the prophets—from you [Muhammad], from Noah, from Abraham, from Moses, from Jesus, son of Mary—We took a solemn pledge from all of them" (33:7).

7. Abi al-'Izz, *Sharh al-'Aqidah al-Tahawiyya*, 505. Theologians further connect the idea of piety with respite since the Qur'anic verse 65:2 states, "God will find a way out for those who are pious and mindful of Him and will provide for them from an unexpected source." Piety thus has material benefits that lead to provisions and resources. Such could be said of Maryam, who, in her moment of need, turned to God and was provided sustenance from the palm tree. Abi al-'Izz, *Sharh al-'Aqidah al-Tahawiyya*, 509.

darkness and into the light." Part of God's support and friendship is providing the believer a spiritual light that guides them amid darkness and uncertainty. Commenting on these verses, early theological texts explain that "God is the protector of his believing servants, he loves them and they love him, he is content with them, and they are content with him. Whoever wages war against his *wali*, then He wages war on them. This *wilaya* is out of his mercy and kindness, not like a creature to another creature where the *wilaya* for another is out of their need."[8] Here, the author differentiates between God's friendship and protection and those of humans and animals, which are often based on self-interest.

The concept of *wilaya* is found in not only Qur'anic verses but also prophetic reports. One example is the famous tradition that explains that God protects the *wali* and eventually guides them as they draw closer to him:

> Verily God has said: "Whosoever shows enmity to a *wali* of Mine, then I have declared war against them. And My servant does not draw near to Me with anything more loved to Me than the religious duties I have obligated upon him. And My servant continues to draw near to me with supererogatory deeds until I Love them. When I Love them, I am their hearing with which they hear, and their sight with which they see, and their hand with which they strike, and their foot with which they walk. Were they to ask [something] of Me, I would surely give it to him; and were they to seek refuge with Me, I would surely grant him refuge."

God eventually begins to guide the *wali*'s actions to the point where they are consistent with God's will and where the *wali*'s prayers and wishes are answered. However, a key point of contention was whether *wilaya* was an elite concept or accessible to all, with early theology texts

8. Abi al-'Izz, *Sharh al-'Aqidah al-Tahawiyya*, 506.

referencing this prophetic tradition and speaking about the idea that "all the believers are the friends of the most Merciful."[9]

## Miracles of the Prophets and Saints

When discussing prophets and *walis*, the topic of miracles appears, as they offered an important way to demonstrate that the figures were unique and had a special connection with God. Miracles are a sign of "transcendent reality beyond this world" and a way to reimagine the world as we normally know it.[10] In the Islamic tradition, miracles are defined as the "disruption of the habitual pattern of creation" and a contradiction of the natural order.[11] Examples of miracles are vast and could contain anything from Musa's staff turning into a snake to a person walking on water or flying in the air.

Muslim scholars generally held that miracles were possible for both prophets and *walis*. Early Islamic creeds, for instance, affirmed both types of miracles, stating, "And God has aided [the prophets] by miracles which contradict the usual course of things" and that "the miracles of the *walīs* are true." However, they distinguished miracles

9. Abi al-'Izz, *Sharh al-'Aqidah al-Tahawiyya*, 506. *Wilaya* is further used not only in reference to God but also between believers themselves. For instance, a Qur'anic verse states that "the believing men and women are supporters (*awliya'*) to one another" (9:71). *Wilaya* is, therefore, a concept that describes one's relationship to God, other believers, and humanity at large. The concepts of *wali* and *wilaya* are also used in Islamic law and Shi'ism. Mawil Y. Izzi Dien and P. E. Walker, "Wilaya," in *Encyclopaedia of Islam, Second Edition*, ed. P. Bearman, Th. Bianquis, C. E. Bosworth, E. van Donzel, and W. P. Heinrichs (E. J. Brill, 2012).

10. For more on the concept of miracles within various religious traditions, see David Weddle, *Miracles: Wonder and Meaning in World Religions* (New York University Press, 2010). As Weddle explains in his introduction (p. 3), the purpose of miracle stories is to make freedom and alternate realities imaginable, possible, and realistic.

11. Miracles were defined as events that disrupt the habitual patterns of creation and are given to authenticate the claims of a prophet. Miracles must come either directly or indirectly from God, they must "break the habit" (*kharq al-'ada*) of the cosmos, no one should be able to duplicate the miracle in kind or quality, and miracles must be unique to the one who claims prophethood.

performed by prophets (*mu'jiza*) and those by *wali*s or saints (*karama*). Those performed by prophets were supposed to prove the sincerity and truthfulness of their message and attract supporters to their cause.[12] Many of the famous biblical and Qur'anic prophets, such as Abraham/Ibrahim, Moses/Musa, and Jesus/'Isa, were believed to have displayed miracles, and the Prophet Muhammad and other Arab prophets were understood to have performed them as well.

In contrast, miracles of saints (*karama*) were supposed to show divine favor, honor, and personal distinction.[13] Unlike the miracles of the prophets, those of saints should not necessarily be publicly declared or shown to support a particular call or missionary work. The miracles of saints are especially important within Sufism, which understood them as "charismatic gifts" that represented a "state of sanctity," blessing (*baraka*), and validation.[14] Within some Sufi circles, miracles could often lead to the veneration of the saints with elaborate gatherings,

---

12. As Wensinck further explains, "A very complete and systematic description occurs in al-Iddji's *Mawakif.* He gives the following definition of *mu'dj̲iza*: it is meant to prove the sincerity of him who pretends to be an apostle of God. Further, he enumerates the following conditions: (1) it must be an act of God; (2) it must be contrary to the usual course of things; (3) contradiction to it must be impossible; (4) it must happen at the hands of him who claims to be an apostle, so that it appears as a confirmation of his sincerity; (5) it must be in conformity with his announcement of it, and the miracle itself must not be a disavowal of his claim (*da'wa*); (6) it must follow on his *da'wa*." A. J. Wensinck, "Mu'djiza," *Encyclopaedia of Islam*, 2nd ed., ed. P. Bearman, Th. Bianquis, C. E. Bosworth, E. van Donzel, and W. P. Heinrichs (E. J. Brill, 2012).

13. As Wensinck explains, "They denote the miracles performed by Allah in order to prove the sincerity of His apostles. The term *karama* [*q.v.*] is used in connection with the saints; it differs from *mu'dj̲iza* in so far as it denotes nothing but a personal distinction granted by God to a saint." Wensinck, "Mu'dj̲iza."

14. The distinction between *karama* and *mu'jiza* was not always clear, especially among Sufi circles. David Thomas, "Miracles in Islam," in *The Cambridge Companion to Miracles*, ed. Graham H. Twelftree (Cambridge University Press, 2011), 212. Thomas's article is especially helpful in understanding miracles within the life of the Prophet Muhammad and Christian-Muslim polemics.

circles, and tombs.[15] However, while many scholars accepted the idea of miracles of saints (*karamas*), many worried that they would eventually compete with or be valued more than the miracles of the prophets.[16] Some scholars tried to limit the miracles of the saints, believing that they could not be greater than those of a prophet, such as 'Isa reviving the dead. Others contended that a proliferation of miracles would be inconceivable and irrational, making true miracles mundane and irrelevant. Moreover, many Islamic philosophers and rationalists had trouble with the concept of miracles, as it challenged their view of causation or that the universe operated within the confines of cause and effect. Some only accepted miracles of the prophets, while others understood miracles within the context of natural phenomena.[17]

## What Was the Status of Maryam?

The above discussion of prophecy and *wilaya* leads to the question of where Maryam would fit within this theological scheme. Muslim scholars struggled to place her within their frameworks, as the Qur'an

---

15. John Esposito, ed., "Karama," in *The Oxford Dictionary of Islam* (Oxford University Press, 2003), 188. The full quote reads, "Refers to charismatic gifts or the capacity to perform miracles, as evidenced by the temporary suspension of natural order through divine intervention. Signifies a state of sanctity and confirms validity of the saint (*wali*) in Sufi circles, encouraging veneration of holy men."

16. Jonathan Brown, "Faithful Dissenters: Sunni Skepticism About the Miracles of Saints," *Journal of Sufi Studies* 1 (2012): 123–168. See also Muhammad Amanullah, "Debate over the Karamah of Allah's Friends," *Arab Law Quarterly* 18, no. 3 (2003): 365–374; Maribel Fierro, "The Polemic About the *karamat al-awliya'* and the Development of Sufism in al-Andalus," *Bulletin of the School of Oriental and African Studies, University of London* 55, no. 2 (1992): 236–249. Fierro speaks about the concern over miracles of the *wali*s in the context of people claiming prophecy in Islamic Spain and North Africa.

17. Isra Yazicioglu, "Redefining the Miraculous: al-Ghazali, Ibn Rushd and Said Nursi on Qur'anic Miracle Stories," *Journal of Qur'anic Studies* 13, no. 2 (2011): 86–108. Yazicioglu discusses how medieval and modern scholars understand Qur'anic miracle stories, especially in the light of a text that deemphasizes miracles, and how they fathomed them in the light of causation and modern science.

and prophetic tradition do not clearly label her a prophet or *wali* (feminine: *waliyya*). Because Maryam seemingly fit multiple categories, she became an important point of theological dispute, debate, and inquiry. Was Maryam a prophet, *wali*, or something else?

For example, scholars were in consensus that Maryam had been given miracles. The Qur'an, for instance, speaks about her receiving fruits out of season, becoming pregnant as a virgin, being comforted during her labor, and having her son speak from the cradle. For those who believed that miracles were the exclusive prerogative of prophets, then Maryam was a prophet, as her miracles were clear, evident, and undisputed. However, for those who contended that *wali*s could receive miracles, then Maryam was an example of the best of the saints or friends of God.[18]

While the Islamic tradition is long and vast,[19] one of the first major attempts to reckon with this issue was the iconoclastic and maverick Andalusian scholar Ibn Hazm (d. 456/1064), who is known for his unique opinions and distinct school of law.[20] In his various works, he argues that women could be prophets and specifically names Maryam as one of them. For Ibn Hazm, prophecy was about divine informing and is distinct from inspiration conjecture, illusions, and astrology. Unlike other types of feelings and inclinations, prophecy was attached to certainty and was not something one could potentially learn. If a woman was spoken to by God—whether through an angel, a dream, or directly—then she should be considered a prophet regardless of her gender.[21] For instance, he regards the biblical and Qur'anic figure Sarah

18. See Fierro, "The Polemic About the *karamat al-awliya'*."

19. See, for instance, the argument that the foundational theologian al-Ash'ari believed in Maryam's prophecy: Halim Calis, "Mary's Prophethood Reassessed: Overlooked Medieval Islamic Perspectives in Contemporary Scholarship," *Religions* 15 (2024): 1–12.

20. This section is adapted from my article "Islamic Mary," 70–102.

21. 'Ali b. Ahmad Ibn Hazm, *al-Ihkam fi usul al-ahkam* (Dar al-Kutub al-'Ilmiyya, 1985), 1: 41. To argue his point, Ibn Hazm looks at the linguistic origins of the word *prophet* in Arabic which he understands to be *informing*.

(Umm Ishaq) as a prophet, as she was informed directly by the angels that she would give birth to Ishaq. Specifically, when Sarah expresses dismay over the fact that she will give birth since she is barren and her husband is old (*shaykh*), the angels directly reply to her, "Do you wonder (*ta'jabin*) about God's affairs?" (11:71). For Ibn Hazm, it is not possible for this angelic statement to be addressed to anyone other than a prophet, as she is directly informed of a divine affair by angels.

In terms of Maryam, Ibn Hazm cites verse 19:19, where the angel Jibril said, "And he said to her 'Verily I am a messenger of your Lord to bestow upon you a pure boy.'" Ibn Hazm exclaims that this is "true prophecy (*al-nabuwwa al-sahiha*), with true revelation and a message (*risala*) from God to her." Here Maryam was spoken to by an angel (Jibril was considered to be the greatest angel) and should be understood to be in the special category of a prophet. Later in the chapter (19:58), the Qur'an states, "These were the prophets God blessed—from the seed of Adam, of those We carried in the Ark with Noah." In Ibn Hazm's reading, "these were the prophets" includes Maryam, and she should not be arbitrarily removed from the categorization.

Ibn Hazm's case does not stop at the Qur'an but continues within the hadith literature. For instance, a prophet tradition states, "Many men have reached completeness (*kamal*), but from the women, completeness is only with Mary, the daughter of 'Imran and Asiya, the daughter of Muzahim, the wife of Pharaoh." Ibn Hazm explains that the Prophet Muhammad specifies Asiya and Maryam as preferred (*tafdil*) over all women who have been given prophecy, even those whose prophecy is attested to by the Qur'an. God says that he has preferred certain prophets over others, and there are certain male prophets, such as Ibrahim and Muhammad, who are also given preference over others. For Ibn Hazm, the "completeness" defined here refers to prophecy.

The argument develops with another Andalusian scholar, al-Qurtubi (d. 671/1273), who builds on the work of Ibn Hazm. In his commentary on the Qur'an, al-Qurtubi argues that Maryam was a prophet (*nabiyya*) and suggests she was superior to other historic prophets and prophets whom she came in contact with. Similar to Ibn Hazm, al-Qurtubi begins his argument by quoting the prophetic hadith: "Many men have reached completeness (*kamal*), but the only women who have reached completeness (*kamal*) are Maryam the daughter of ʿImran and Asiya the wife of Pharaoh." Here al-Qurtubi explains that "completeness" could mean many things such as "reaching the end" or "wholeness."[22] Completeness is also relative to absolute completeness belonging to God. For al-Qurtubi, there is no doubt that the most complete human beings are the prophets and then the friends of God and saints (*awliyaʾ*) mentioned above.[23] However, prophecy was not simply related to "completeness" but a direct communication with the divine.

Al-Qurtubi then cites a series of prophet traditions (many of which were discussed in the previous chapter) as evidence of the exalted nature of Maryam. The first states that "the best women of all of creation are four: Maryam the daughter of ʿImran, Asiya the daughter of Muzahim the wife of Pharaoh, Khadija the daughter of Khuwaylid (the wife of Muhammad), and Fatima the daughter of Muhammad." A second tradition states, "The best women of Paradise are Khadija the daughter of Khuwaylid and Fatima the daughter of Muhammad, Mary the daughter of ʿImran, and Asiya the daughter of Muzahim the wife of Pharaoh." Another similar narration states, "The mistresses of the women of Paradise after Maryam are Fatima and Khadija."

Al-Qurtubi then states his own opinion that it is evident from the Qur'an and the hadiths that Maryam is the best of all the women, from Eve to the last woman who will stand on the day of judgment, as the angels had informed her of God's revelation, and all of the prophets were (divinely) informed. Thus, according to al-Qurtubi, she is a prophet, and a prophet is greater than a saint or a friend of God; she is absolutely the

22. Muhammad b. Ahmad al-Qurtubi, *al-Jamiʿ li-ahkam al-Qur'an: wa'l-mubayyin li-ma tadammanahu min al-sunna wa-ay al-Furqan*, ed. ʿAbd Allah b. ʿAbd al-Muhsin Turki and Muhammad Ridwan ʿIrqsusi (Mu'assasat al-Risāla, 2006), 5: 126.

23. After the friends of God, al-Qurtubi mentions the truthful ones (*siddiqin*), the martyrs or witnesses (*shuhadaʾ*), and the righteous (*salihin*).

best of all women, from the beginning to the end of time. Al-Qurtubi goes on to explain that God selected her and gave her what he did not give other women, in that Jibril (*ruh al-qudus*) spoke to her, appeared before her, blew into her shirt, and came close to her to do so; he did not do this to any other woman.[24]

Al-Qurtubi then begins a new section in which he speaks to the idea of Maryam being *siddiqa*, or "sincere and truthful," and implies that she was, in fact, greater than even other *male* prophets (the term will be defined further below). The Qur'an further testifies to her virtuous and truthful nature, saying in Q. 5:75 that Jesus's mother was *siddiqa*. In Q. 66:12, the Qur'an says that Maryam accepted the truth (*saddaqat*) of her Lord's words and scriptures: She was truly devout (*qanitin*) [i.e., the verse testifies to her being *siddiqa* in that she affirmed the words of glad tidings and that she is devout (*qunut*)]. Al-Qurtubi explains that Maryam is *siddiqa* because she accepted God's plan for her and did not ask for any sign as Zakariyya did. In contrast to Maryam, when Zakariyya was given the glad tidings of a child, he observed his old age and responded, "How am I going to have a son when my wife is barren?" and thus asked for a sign. Maryam, on the other hand, when given the glad tidings of a child, explained that she was a virgin and that no man had touched her. When she was then told (in Q. 19:21) that this is what God has decreed, she was content with the answer. She did not ask for a sign because she knew God's power and ability in this affair. Al-Qurtubi seems unable to contain himself and exclaims, "Which woman from all of the worlds—from the daughters of Adam—has these virtues (*manaqib*)!"

In summary, like Ibn Hazm, al-Qurtubi believed that Maryam was a prophet because she spoke to God's angels, specifically Jibril, and held an exalted place because she affirmed God's message. To him, being a

---

24. Here we see al-Qurtubi's Sunni bias, in that he holds Maryam in a greater light than the Prophet's family, specifically his daughter Fatima. As will be discussed later in this chapter, there have been long and extensive debates within Shi'ism regarding whether Maryam or Fatima was considered to be the best of all women, with many holding them at the same level or Fatima as higher.

prophet did not necessarily involve playing a public role, as we will see later with other scholars, but was rather a function of one's relationship with God: A prophet had the closest station to God and had direct communication with God or his angels. However, al-Qurtubi differs from Ibn Hazm in that he sees Maryam in a special light and accords her a higher rank than other female Qur'anic figures. For instance, the Qur'anic Sarah saw and spoke to the angels who gave her and Ibrahim the glad tidings of Ishaq, but the angels did not come close to her and blow their "spirit" into her. Similarly, God revealed to the mother of Musa that she should put him into the Nile, but no angel appeared to her and spoke directly to her. For al-Qurtubi, Maryam has a special place among all women because of Jibril appearing before her, speaking to her, and blowing his spirit into her. She is further *siddiqa* because she affirmed God's message and was truthful, a label not given to other women. Even more importantly, al-Qurtubi does not only see Maryam as the best of all women but also imply that she is better than other male prophets such as Zakariyya, who asked for a sign from God, while Maryam did not. The fact that Maryam can be ranked among the exceptional prophets is confirmed to him by the prophetic hadith that lists her among the most famous messengers, which include Ibrahim and Musa. Al-Qurtubi even compares Maryam to Muhammad in that they are labeled in unique ways that speak to their exalted spiritual states. Maryam is thus the best of all women and one of the superior Islamic prophets.

Modern feminist scholars consider the ideas of Ibn Hazm and al-Qurtubi protofeminist, as they see their views as supported by Islamic feminists who would eventually emerge in the twentieth century. They both do not discount Maryam for being a prophet because she was a female and didn't necessarily have an issue ranking her above other male figures.[25] However, Ibn Hazm's and Qurtubi's views could result from more of their definition of prophecy than necessarily their belief in the capacity of females and support of female religious leadership. Moreover, it is noteworthy that both scholars emerged from an Andalusian context

25. Abboud, "'Idhan Maryam Nabiyya,' 183–196.

where their Christian surroundings could have influenced them.[26] Andalusian Muslims saw the reverence of Christians toward Mary, which may have led them to think more closely about Maryam's status and her role in Islamic thought and culture.

## Maryam Not as a Prophet but as a *Siddiqa*

Not all Muslim thinkers considered Maryam to be a prophet. Arguably the most influential refutation of Maryam being a prophet would come from the Damascene scholar Ibn Kathir (d. 774/1373). While Ibn Kathir was open to the idea that Qur'anic women received revelation, he was against the idea that they were prophets, as they are never called such in the Qur'an, and the majority opinion maintained that prophecy was exclusive to men. Ibn Kathir's argument against female prophecy first appears in his commentary on Q. 5:75: "The Messiah, son of Mary, was only a messenger; other messengers had come and gone before him; his mother was sincere and truthful (*siddiqa*)." He contends that the verse is evidence that Maryam was a *siddiqa*, and this honorific was her "highest position and [the verse] is evidence that she was not a prophet as Ibn Hazm and others falsely claim."[27] He then explains Ibn Hazm's argument that Sarah, Jochebed (Umm Musa), and Maryam were prophets because of direct divine communication. Sarah and Maryam, in particular, communicated directly with angels. Ibn Kathir states that the majority opinion is that God only sends men as prophets (12:109), and he refers to early theologians who believed that there was consensus on the issue.

However, it is in his commentary on Q. 12:109 (stating that God has sent "men" [*rijal*] as messengers) that Ibn Kathir presents his most extensive argument that prophecy is exclusive to men. He

26. See Maribel Fierro, "Women as Prophets," in *Writing the Feminine: Women in Arab Sources*, ed. Randi Deguilhem and Manuela Marín (I. B. Tauris, 2002), 183–198.

27. Ibn Kathir, *Tafsir al-Qur'an al-'azim*, ed. Hikmat Bashir Yasin (Dar Ibn al-Jawzi li'l-Nashr wa'l-Tawzi', 2015/2016), 3: 441.

begins his commentary by saying that God "informs [us] that He sent messengers among the men and not women, and this is the statement and view (*qawl*) of the majority of the scholars." The fact that Ibn Kathir launches into his commentary on the verse with this statement is a strong indication that the debate over whether women could be prophets was very much alive and was something he felt compelled to respond to and refute. Ibn Kathir proceeds to explain that women were not given "a revelation of legislation" (*wahy tashri'*), suggesting that women could receive "revelation" (*wahy*) but not that of the prophetic kind. Ibn Kathir continues that "some scholars" falsely claim that Sarah, Jochebed (Umm Musa), and Maryam were prophets and base their argument on the Qur'anic narratives about these women. Even though Ibn Kathir is not explicit on who "these scholars" are, he is undoubtedly speaking about Ibn Hazm (who he explicitly names earlier in his commentary on Q. 5:75) and his argument of female prophecy. Ibn Kathir believes that these verses demonstrate the women's exalted rank, but that this does not mean they were prophets. He explains that if somebody wants to say they are prophets as a way to speak to their honorable status, then there is no doubt about that (that they are honorable). However, the question remains as to whether they followed the model and path of prophecy.

Ibn Kathir also states that he follows the Sunni orthodoxy, believing in the legacy of Muhammad (*sunna*) and the consensus (*ahl al-sunna wa'l-jama'a*) that there are no prophets among women. Rather, they are *siddiqat* (plural form), as God states in Q. 5:75. If Maryam were a prophet, then it would be explicitly mentioned as a way to speak about her honor and exalted stature. However, she is ascribed only with the noble rank of *siddiqa*, according to the text of the Qur'an.

Ibn Kathir's comments are significant because he entertains the idea that the Qur'anic women were prophets as an honorific but did not believe that they followed the footsteps and path of the male prophets, who called their people to a particular message. Rather, Ibn Kathir considers these Qur'anic women to be *siddiqat* on the basis that the Qur'an does not explicitly say that any of the women were prophets but rather labels Maryam as a *siddiqa*. Moreover, the fact that Ibn Kathir links the discussion of female prophecy to the foundational theologians and Sunni orthodoxy demonstrates how the issue was increasingly becoming a theological one. Ibn Kathir's reference to Sunni orthodoxy and consensus was another way to marginalize Ibn Hazm and his opinion on female prophecy; he admits there were some scholars who believed in female prophecy, but they were the minority, and the majority opinion states that only men could be prophets.

In his "Stories of the Prophets" (*Qisas al-anbiya'*), Ibn Kathir echoes his Qur'anic commentary and makes sure to note in three different places that Sarah, Jochebed (the mother of Musa), and Maryam were not prophets but rather *siddiqat*. In the first instance, he makes the general statement that "some scholars" believed that the three were prophets, but in the latter two passages, he names and openly critiques Ibn Ḥazm. However, it is through the example of Maryam that Ibn Kathir expands most on the idea that prophecy is exclusive to men. In his explanation of Q. 3:42, "We chose her among all women," Ibn Kathir explains that even if Maryam were a prophet, as Ibn Hazm and others falsely claim, she would be considered a better female prophet than either Jochebed or Sarah. The statement is remarkable because Ibn Kathir once again entertains the idea that Maryam could have been a prophet, even though he did not believe that was the case. He then forthrightly states that the majority opinion of scholars and the consensus was that women were not among the prophets. Nonetheless, the highest position among women (*maqam*) is held by Maryam. He also notes that Maryam is associated (in prophetic hadiths) with Asiya, Khadija, and Fatima. After stating their names, Ibn Kathir praises and prays for them: "May God be pleased with all of them and grant them happiness."

The fact that Ibn Kathir spends the most time in this section on Maryam, in making his case against the prophecy of women, suggests he believed that the argument for her prophecy was strong and convincing. The verses that recount how God chose her and an angel spoke directly to her are profound and could be interpreted as indicative of her having prophetic status. However, Ibn Kathir prefers the Qur'anic title of *siddiqa* given to Mary and believes instead that she was the best woman of all time. While the idea of male superiority played a role in Ibn Kathir's analysis, it does not explicitly appear in his refutation of Ibn Hazm.

Moreover, Ibn Kathir does not argue that women are ineligible for prophecy because they lack purity (because they menstruate) or that they are unable to play a public role. For instance, some early theological texts affirm that prophets could only be male since "femininity contradicts 'being sent.'"[28] Males could be "well-known so as to proclaim the message," while females were required to "conceal" themselves.[29] Thus, it was inconceivable for a female to be a prophet, as prophets were expected to have a public and proselytizing role. Rather, for Ibn Kathir, the core issue was what the fundamental texts of the Qur'an and hadith said about Maryam's status, which was that she was a *siddiqa*. In fact, Ibn Kathir attempts to elevate Maryam to the highest level in his paradigm of "the best woman of all time." Contrary to other scholars, Ibn Kathir believed that Maryam was even better than Muhammad's wife Khadija and his daughter Fatima. He does recognize the opinion of female prophecy as a minority one but maintains the position held by Sunni orthodoxy that prophecy was exclusive to men.

Indeed, Ibn Kathir's categorization of Maryam as a *siddiqa* is reminiscent of the term *wali* mentioned above. Maryam was truthful to her word and therefore guided and protected by God. While Ibn Kathir did not believe that Maryam was a prophet, he nonetheless held her in high esteem and believed that she was a model worthy of emulation and praise. Similarly, other commentators also denied Maryam's prophecy but considered her miracles as examples of those of the *wali*s and saints. For instance, the famous commentator al-Razi (d. 606/1210) states that Jibril approaching Maryam "was a miracle (*karama*) for her, and that is

28. Nur al-Din al-Sabuni, *An Introduction to Islamic Theology (al-Bidayah fi usul al-din)*, trans. and ed. Faraz Khan (Zaytuna Institute; Sandala, 2020), 166.

29. Faraz Khan, the translator and editor of the work *An Introduction to Islamic Theology*, comments here "that is out of modesty and social etiquette."

permissible for those who believe in the miracles of the saints (*awliya'*)." For al-Razi, Maryam was not a prophet, but rather her miracles indicate that she was a *wali*, which was also the position of various theological schools. Her miracles could additionally be connected with the coming of 'Isa or associated with the prophecy of Zakariyya.[30]

It is important to note that much of these debates occur with Qur'anic exegesis (*tafsir*) and not theological treatises or introductory texts. Qur'anic commentators (*mufassirin*) had to contend with Qur'anic verses where Maryam was said to be chosen, approached by an angel, and given distinct miracles. The commentators saw these verses as similar to others about prophets and *wali*s and were compelled to differentiate between the two. In contrast, theological texts spoke in general terms about prophets and *wali*s and did not necessarily mention Maryam because she was not explicitly categorized as either.[31] Theologians, for instance, spoke about prophecy in the context of more well-known and recognized prophets, such as Muhammad and Ibrahim, and did not delve into debates regarding those who were not as prominent.

## Maryam Within Shi'i Thought

While Sunni theologians debated the status of Maryam as a prophet, Shi'i groups maintained that 'Ali (the cousin and son-in-law of the Prophet) was the closest companion to the Prophet Muhammad and should have succeeded him as caliph after he died.[32] Shi'i commentators and theologians thus understood Maryam as "the best woman of *her time*," as they saw Fatima—who was the daughter of Muhammad,

30. Fakhr al-Din al-Razi, *al-Tafsir al-kabir*, ed. Sayyid 'Umran, 32 vols. (Dar al-Hadith, 2012), 2: 257.

31. Perhaps they don't mention Maryam by name, but they could be alluding to her in their defining why a woman cannot be a prophet.

32. For more on this topic, see Mary Thurlkill, *Chosen Among Women: Mary and Fatima in Medieval Christianity and Shiite Islam* (University of Notre Dame Press, 2007); J. D. McAuliffe, "Chosen of All Women: Mary and Fatima in Qur'anic Exegesis," *Islamochristiana* 7 (1981): 19–28.

the wife of 'Ali, and the mother of subsequent imams—as being the best of *all women*. Fatima therefore plays a "crucial link between the Prophet, Ali, and the Imams." She further "has mythical status in the Shi'i tradition" as "she is celebrated (as she is in the Sunni tradition) for her closeness to her father, the Prophet, as well as for her piety, humility, and poverty, and devotion as a wife and mother."[33] Shi'i scholars frequently compared Fatima to Maryam, elevating Fatima's status and suggesting that Maryam's miracles were connected to other prophets.[34]

For instance, the Shi'i commentator al-Tusi (459–460/1066–7) provides two explanations regarding the question of the angels appearing to Maryam and whether she was a prophet. The first is that the appearance was a miracle for Zakariyya, not Maryam, because "she was not a prophet," based on verse 12:109 cited above.[35] Second, the miracles she witnessed are similar to those foreshadowing the prophecy of Muhammad, such as the clouds shading him on his journeys, and thus are more of a sign of the coming of 'Isa than of Maryam being a prophet herself. Moreover, within Shi'i theology, "the appearance of a miracle is permissible on the hands of the saints (*awliya'*) or righteous"[36] and are a way to affirm the truth of those who perform them regardless of whether they are a prophet, an imam, or righteous. Thus, for al-Tusi, miracles are not necessarily a condition of prophecy but rather more of a demonstration that the person is virtuous and truthful. In terms of Maryam, the miracles she witnessed and performed did not mean

33. Maria Dakake, "Re-reading the Quranic Maryam as a Mystic in Nusrat Amin's Makhzan-i 'irfan," in *Islamic Thought and the Art of Translation Texts and Studies in Honor of William C. Chittick and Sachiko Murata*, ed. Mohammed Rustom (Brill, 2023), 83.

34. As we will see later, modern Shi'i women would elevate the status of Maryam, seeing her as an important figure in her own right.

35. Abi Ja'far Muhammad b. al-Hasan al-Tusi, *al-Tibyan fi tafsir al-Qur'an*, ed. Ahmad Habib Qasir al-'Amili (Dar Ihya' al-Turath al-'Arabi, 1409/1989), 2: 457.

36. Al-Tusi, *al-Tibyan fi tafsir al-Qur'an*, 2: 457.

she was a prophet but rather fit into other categories of the righteous defined above.[37]

Drawing on similar sources, the Shiʿi commentator al-Tabarsi (d. 565/1169–70) interprets verse 3:42 as Maryam being the best woman of *her time* and asserts that Fatima was the best woman of *all time*, with him sending prayers for her father (Muhammad), husband (ʿAli), and children (Hasan and Husayn).[38] Despite his reverence for Maryam, al-Tabarsi maintained that Fatima was the best woman, partly because of her relationship to the Prophet Muhammad, the imam and caliph ʿAli, and her sons and subsequent imams Hasan and Husayn.[39] To support his claim, al-Tabarsi cites the prophetic hadith that "Khadija was preferred in my nation (*umma*) just like Maryam was preferred as a woman in her time (*nisaʾ al-ʿalimin*)." Here, al-Tabarsi understands that Maryam was preferred in her generation, just like Khadija was in hers. However, Fatima is considered to be the best woman of all time for the various reasons listed above. Moreover, al-Tabarsi observes that there are two instances in which verse 3:42 notes that Maryam was "chosen": "The angels said to Mary: 'Mary, God *has chosen* you and made you pure: He has *truly chosen* you among women." Here al-Tabarsi understands the first use to mean that she was "chosen" among the progeny of the prophets and the second to mean she was "chosen" to give birth to ʿIsa. Therefore, the end of the verse, "He has truly chosen you of all women,"

37. Al-Tusi also suggests that verse 3:42 could have been conveyed to her through Zakariyya and not directly by an angel. This argument would support the claim that Maryam was not a prophet because an angel did not communicate directly with her.

38. As Thurlkill notes, "Fatima's presence among the *ahl al-bayt* ultimately depended on her role as Muhammad's daughter, ʿAli's wife, and the Imams' mother." Thurkill, *Chosen Among Women*, 3. Moreover, as Dakake explains, the comparison between Fatima and Maryam "raises the thornier issue, for Shiʿis, of how to understand the Quranic assertion that Maryam was chosen and preferred above 'all women.'" Dakake, "Re-reading the Quranic Maryam," 84.

39. Husayn, in particular, is remembered as a martyr in Karbala, where he stood against the tyranny and oppression of the caliph Yazid despite the overwhelming odds against him.

should only be read in the context of her time in that she was "chosen" to give birth to the prophet 'Isa.[40]

Other parallels between Maryam and Fatima exist, especially in their honorifics and birthing stories. Fatima is sometimes referred to as the "greater Maryam" (*Maryam al-kubra*), and some Shi'i hadith literature associates the title with the Prophet Muhammad, as it was a way in which he referred to his daughter.[41] The title praises Maryam as an exemplary woman but asserts that Fatima is the "greater Maryam," or the superior woman, and continues the idea that Fatima is the "best woman of all time." The tradition further specifically compares Fatima with Maryam and not any other women. Despite there being many women who were devout, observant, and ascetic—many of which are described in the Qur'an—the tradition is intentional in comparing Fatima to Maryam because both were chosen by God, with Shi'is believing that they were protected from sin (*ma'sum*).[42] Moreover, implicit in the comparison is their role of pious mothers who came from righteous families and birthed prophets and imams. Yet the tradition does not say that Fatima "is like Maryam" but rather that she is "greater."

One of the reasons why Shi'i theologians maintained that Fatima was "greater" was her relationship to the Prophet Muhammad. While Zakariyya and Hana were the caretakers of Maryam, the Prophet Muhammad and his wife Khadija were the ones who raised Fatima.[43] In Islamic theology, the Prophet Muhammad is greater than the Prophet Zakariyya and, therefore, the better caretaker. Fatima's character and nature came from the Prophet Muhammad, and "her light emerged from the light of lights."[44] Fatima was the most similar person to the Prophet Muhammad, and she resembled him in her physical attributes,

40. Al-Tusi, cited above, makes this point as well and references similar sources.

41. Muhammad Baqir al-Khajuri, *al-Khasa'is al-Fatimiyya* (al-Sharif al-Radi, 1959), 220.

42. Al-Khajuri, *al-Khasa'is al-Fatimiyya*, 249.

43. Al-Khajuri, *al-Khasa'is al-Fatimiyya*, 429.

44. Al-Khajuri, *al-Khasa'is al-Fatimiyya*, 429.

character, mannerisms, words, and actions.[45] Nonetheless, even though the title "the greater Maryam" favors Fatima, it presents both women as exceptional and worthy of emulation.

Other traditions typologically connect Fatima to Maryam regarding birth and miracles. One story emerged when the Prophet Muhammad ascended to the heavens in the miraculous "Night Journey and Ascension" (*al-isra' wa'l-mi'raj*). The tradition narrates that the angel Jibril brought the Prophet Muhammad into the sixth heaven, where he saw a tree of light with two angels next to it. On the tree were some dates, so he ate one of them, which became sperm. When he returned to earth, he had intercourse with his wife Khadija, and she became pregnant with Fatima. When Khadija was pregnant with Fatima, the unborn child comforted her, consoling her about the ill-treatment she received at the hands of the people of Mecca. The story links Fatima with the Qur'anic 'Isa as comforting their pregnant mothers in times of difficulty and hardship.[46] It could also connect Muhammad and Maryam, as they both ate dates from a palm tree before the birth of their righteous children.[47]

A similar tradition parallels Khadija and Maryam in that when Khadija was giving birth to Fatima, the people of Quraysh refused to help her, and she began to give birth in isolation. As her labor began, four tall women appeared before her, making her afraid and agitated. Then one of them comforted her, saying, "Don't be afraid Khadija; we are sent to you by God to be your helpers."[48] The four of them then introduced themselves: Sarah, the wife of Ibrahim; Asiya, the daughter of Muzahim (wife of Pharaoh); Maryam, the daughter of 'Imran; and Kulthum, the sister of Musa, the son of 'Imran. They stationed themselves around Khadija as midwives and helped clean and dress the newborn and blessed daughter Fatima.

---

45. Al-Khajuri, *al-Khasa'is al-Fatimiyya*, 430.

46. Potentially Qur'an 19:24–26.

47. McAuliffe, "'Chosen Among All Women,'" 26.

48. McAuliffe, "'Chosen Among All Women,'" 26.

The tradition imagines Khadija in a similar plight to Maryam's in giving birth in seclusion and Fatima as a type of 'Isa who has a blessed birth that will bring glad tidings into the world. It further connects Khadija and Fatima to the great Abrahamic women of the past: Sarah, Asiya, Kulthum, and Maryam. Each woman had helped with either the birth or rearing of a historic prophet and righteous individual—Sarah with Isaac/Ishaq, Asiya and Kulthum with Moses/Musa, and Maryam with 'Isa. Thus, when Khadija is in a state of despair and rejection, the great and righteous female caretakers of the past emerge to help her through her labor. Their emergence further seems to represent an angelic presence and is reminiscent of Qur'anic depictions of the interaction between prophets and angels. For instance, in the famous biblical and Qur'anic story, angels appear before Ibrahim for the annunciation of Ishaq. In the Qur'anic version, their appearance makes Ibrahim frightened, but they comfort him by saying, "Don't be afraid" and bringing the glad tidings of Ishaq.[49]

A final story connects Fatima and Maryam in their miracles, specifically receiving provisions from God. The Prophet Muhammad reportedly did not have any food, having not found any with his wives. He then came to the house of his daughter Fatima to inquire if she had any food, and she mentioned she did. Earlier that day, a neighbor had sent her some food for her husband and sons, but she preemptively put it away, "knowing presciently that this food was divinely intended for the Prophet."[50] When the Prophet arrived, she immediately sent her son to fetch some of the food and put it in a container. When Muhammad opened it, it miraculously overflowed with food.[51] When the Prophet asks where the food had come from, Fatima responds, citing Maryam's words (Q: 3:37), "It is from God. Truly He provides for whomever He will without reckoning." The Prophet replies, "By thanking God for allowing him to witness the miracle that Zakariyya saw from

49. Qur'an 11:70.

50. Dakake, "Re-reading the Quranic Maryam," 84.

51. Dakake explains that the account "also bears parallels with the Gospel story of the loaves and the fishes." Dakake, "Re-reading the Quranic Maryam," 84.

Maryam."[52] The tradition places Fatima in the place of Maryam and the Prophet Muhammad in that of Zakariyya. Fatima even uses Maryam's words to remind the Prophet Muhammad of a spiritual lesson: Provisions come only from God.

In summary, the various Shi'i traditions imagine the great women in the Prophet's life, specifically Khadija and Fatima, in the place of Maryam. Whether it is giving birth or performing miracles, the women around the Prophet Muhammad are portrayed in the model of Maryam in seeking help and receiving divine support. However, it is Fatima who is the superior woman, as she connects the Prophet Muhammad, 'Ali, and the subsequent imams.

## Conclusion

Maryam did not fit neatly into Islamic theological categories and continues to occupy an exceptional religious and spiritual space. She shares elements of a prophet in that she was directly communicated to by an angel and mentioned in the Qur'an alongside other prophets. However, unlike other prophets, she did not actively preach nor come with a written scripture. Moreover, she shares attributes of a *wali* in that God guided her and defends her when she is attacked and maligned. Yet some Muslim theologians had trouble with just categorizing her as a *wali* because she had direct communication with God, especially through one of his most prominent and revered angels. Similar to both a prophet and *wali*, Maryam received miracles with the fruits provided to her out of season and gave birth to 'Isa as a virgin. However, miracles were not the exclusive province of prophets or saints but rather understood to demonstrate the favor and truthfulness of the righteous.

Scholars further struggled to fit her within other hierarchies, especially that of the best of women. Many felt she was the best woman of all time based on the Qur'an verse 3:42 and the facts that God spoke directly to her and Jibril blew his spirit into her. Despite her being a

52. Dakake, "Re-reading the Quranic Maryam," 84.

non-Arab and a figure emerging from a Christian historiography, many Muslim theologians considered her to be the most exemplary woman, even more than Muhammad's first wife and supporter, Khadija. However, others, especially Shiʿi ones, ranked her below Fatima, who was the daughter of the Prophet Muhammad; the wife of the Prophet's cousin and first imam, ʿAli; and the mother of the subsequent imams Hasan and Husayn. Thus, while medieval theologians were in consensus that Maryam was praiseworthy and a model to emulate, they struggled to place her within their theological schemes and hierarchics. Maryam remains a special figure who occupies a unique place within Islamic theology and belief.

CHAPTER FOUR

# Maryam and Mysticism

While Maryam plays an important role in Islamic scripture, she also plays a role in the mystical sources or the "unseen." The mystical sources focus more on Maryam's spiritual dimension rather than her place within a particular category, hierarchy, or list. Mystics and divine seekers saw Maryam as a model for emulation and strove to follow her example in terms of piety, miracles, and reliance on God. Mysticism complements the scriptural sources by finding spiritual meaning within them and providing practical lessons for the believer.

## Islamic Mysticism

Mysticism represents the otherworldly or the "unseen" (*ghayb*) and is part of the human desire to connect with the divine. As the great scholar of mysticism Annemarie Schimmel explains, "Mysticism contains something mysterious, not to be reached by ordinary means or by intellectual effort, is understood from the root common to the words mystic and mystery, the Greek *myein*, 'to close the eyes.'"[1] Mystics are further "concerned above all with 'the mysteries of the Kingdom of Heaven'" and are divine seekers looking toward the heavenly realm.[2] Schimmel further clarifies, "For the reality that is the goal of the mystic, and is ineffable, cannot be understood or explained by any normal mode of perception; neither philosophy nor

1. Annemarie Schimmel, *Mystical Dimensions of Islam* (University of North Carolina Press, 1975), 3.

2. Martin Lings, *What Is Sufism?* (George Allen and Unwin, 1975), 12.

reason can reveal it. Only the wisdom of the heart, gnosis, may give insight into some of its aspects."[3] Thus, mysticism is unique from the other aspects we covered, such as those dealing with the Qur'an, prophetic tradition, and theology. The first two, in particular, are text-based and analyzed through the use of hermeneutics, philology, and historical and linguistic tools. However, while mysticism has produced texts, its focus is on the heart and, therefore, the immaterial, miraculous, and unseen.[4]

In Islam, the word *Sufism* is frequently associated with mysticism, leading to the question of how "Islamic" the concept is. It is important to note that "Sufis view their thought and way of life as Qur'anic in every sense"[5] and find justifications for their beliefs and practices in key foundational Islamic sources, such as the Qur'an and Sunna.[6] The Qur'an describes the world as miraculous and blessed but also potentially deceptive, transient, and distracting from the final abode.[7] Verses describe God as "near" and even closer than one's jugular vein, ready at any moment to support the believer and believing community (2:115, 186; 50:16). Others speak about God being wherever the believer turns (2:115) and God as "light" (24:35), guiding whomever he wills to that light. Some verses even praise the asceticism and God-fearing of

3. Schimmel, *Mystical Dimensions of Islam*, 4.

4. For more on how Sufism was viewed within Western scholarship and Orientalism, see Carl Ernst, *Sufism: An Introduction to the Mystical Tradition of Islam* (Shambhala, 2011).

5. In his book *Early Islamic Mysticism: Sufi, Qur'an, Miraj, Poetic and Theological Writings*, Michael Sells makes it a point to start by speaking about the Qur'an and how Sufis build off the scripture. Michael Sells, *Early Islamic Mysticism: Sufi, Qur'an, Miraj, Poetic and Theological Writings* (Paulist Press, 1996), 29. For more on Sufism and the Qur'an, see also Alexander Knysh, "Sufism and the Qur'an," in *Encyclopaedia of the Qur'an*, ed. Johanna Pink (E. J. Brill, 2023).

6. Alexander Knysh, *Sufism: A New History of Islamic Mysticism* (Princeton University Press, 2017), 15.

7. Knysh, *Sufism*, 15.

Christian monks, which became a model for early Muslim ascetics.[8] Specifically to Maryam, there is an entire chapter named after her, which contains "one of the more dramatic and beloved discussions of a female figure in the Qur'an."[9] The story of Maryam and the Qur'anic chapter would thus become a paradigm for later Sufis, especially women, who were drawn to her spiritual and mystical nature.

Sufis also reference prophet traditions such as this popular one, which suggests a mystical union between the individual and God: "When my servant draws near to me through obligatory and free devotions . . . I become the hearing with which he hears, the seeing with which he sees, the hands with which he touches, the feet with which he walks, and the tongue with which he speaks."[10] While the exact meaning of the tradition is debated, it signals that God guides those he loves and directs their limbs and actions. Based on this prophetic hadith and others, Sufis frequently tried to model themselves after the Prophet Muhammad and his prophetic legacy (Sunna) to seek divine guidance and blessings.

However, it is important to note that Sufism developed over time, like other Islamic disciplines such as hadith and theology. The term *Sufism* may have been alien to the first Muslims and early generations, but its roots are found in the early ascetic practices of the Prophet Muhammad, as well as his companions and successors. Despite the various obstacles and challenges, Islamic mysticism and Sufism have evolved and survived throughout the centuries and into modernity. The answer may lie in Sufism's self-disciplining nature, on the one hand, and "its ability to offer a loftier, transcendent meaning to human life on the

---

8. As Knysh explains, "As regards asceticism-mysticism, the Qur'anic references to monks and their beliefs and practices, which have been cited above, are evidence enough that monasticism and Christianity more generally were already part and parcel of the Qur'an's symbolic universe." Knysh, *Sufism*, 22.

9. Sells, *Early Islamic Mysticism*, 34.

10. Sells, *Early Islamic Mysticism*, 22.

other."[11] Maryam has always been important in offering that "loftier" ideal and means to come close to the transcendent.

## The Feminine Branch of Islam: Sufism and Women

While women have been attracted to the various Islamic sciences,[12] there is a strand of scholarship that argues that Sufism was more favorable toward women and female attributes and characteristics.[13] The Sufis "were well aware of the positive aspects of womanhood," and many Sufis did not see females as negative, even believing that certain feminine attributes were praiseworthy.[14] Shrines for females exist throughout Muslim lands, and in modern times, the teachers of Sufism and directors of its various centers are often women.[15] It can be even said that "Sufism was more favorable to the development of feminine activities than were other branches of Islam."[16] In contrast to other dis-

11. Knysh, *Sufism*, 32.

12. Asma Sayeed, *Women and the Transmission of Religious Knowledge in Islam* (Cambridge University Press, 2013).

13. This section of the chapter is adapted from the blog by Younus Y. Mirza, "The Deputy of Maryam—The Mystic Rabiʿa al-ʿAdawiyya in Light of the Qur'anic Mary," *Maydan* (2023).

14. Schimmel, *Mystical Dimensions of Islam*, 435.

15. Schimmel, *Mystical Dimensions of Islam*, 435; Margaret Smith, "Rabiʿa the Mystic," in *Middle Eastern Women Speak*, ed. Elizabeth Warnock Fernea and Basima Qattan Bezirgan (University of Texas Press, 1977), 37. For more on women and Sufi shrines and singers, see Shemeem Burney Abbas, *The Female Voice in Sufi Ritual: Devotional Practices of Pakistan and India* (University of Texas Press, 2002).

16. Schimmel, *Mystical Dimensions of Islam*, 426. This theme is echoed in the literature on Sufism and women, which views Sufism as one of the few strands of Islam that retains equality and respect for women. Camille Adams Helminski, *Women of Sufism: A Hidden Treasure: Writings and Stories of Mystic Poets, Scholars and Saints* (Shambhala, 2003), xxiii. However, for a counterview to this arguments see, Codou Bop, "Roles and the Position of Women in Sufi Brotherhoods in Senegal," *Journal of the American Academy of Religion* 73, no. 4 (December, 2005): 1099–1119. In her article, Bop speaks primarily about the Sufi tariqa system rather than the Sufi

ciplines, "many women found the Sufi path to be a realm in which their participation and even original contributions were eventually validated, if not always immediately accepted."[17]

Female religious figures have often been celebrated among Sufis. For instance, Sufis have noted the Qur'anic example of Zulaykha, who fell in love with the young Yusuf to the point that she threw herself on him and cut her hands in his presence. For many Sufis, the story exemplified the love of the divine and the righteous that endured through pain, sacrifice, and hardship.[18] Sufis "particularly loved Mary, Maryam, the immaculate mother who gave birth to the spiritual child Jesus. . . . She is often taken as the symbol of the spirit that receives divine inspiration and thus becomes pregnant with the divine light."[19] Maryam was seen as someone who came near to God through her devotional deeds, and thus God guided her actions and

---

mystical path in general. For more on women in Sufi orders, see Marta Dominguez Diaz, *Women in Sufism: Female Religiosities in a Transnational Order* (Routledge, 2015). Rkia Cornell also argues that classical Sufism was often more egalitarian than modern forms. Muḥammad ibn al-Ḥusayn Sulamī, *Early Sufi Women: Dhikr an-niswa al-muta'abbidāt aṣ-Ṣūfiyyāt*, trans. Rkia Cornell (Fons Vitae, 1999), 20. See also the work of Nelly Amri.

17. Maria Dakake, "Walking upon the Path of God Like Men?: Women and the Feminine in the Islamic Mystical Tradition," *Sophia: A Journal of Traditional Studies* 8, no. 2 (2002): 132. Nonetheless, Laury Silvers emphasizes that Muslim women's spirituality operates within patriarchal norms. Laury Silvers, "Early Pious, Mystic Sufi Women," in *The Cambridge Companion to Sufism*, ed. Lloyd Ridgeon (Cambridge University Press, 2015), 52.

18. Schimmel, *Mystical Dimensions of Islam*, 429. As Schimmel writes, "The woman completely lost in her love of Joseph/Yusuf is a fine symbol for the enrapturing power of love, expressed by the mystic in the contemplation of divine beauty revealed in human form."

19. Schimmel, *Mystical Dimensions of Islam*, 429. Schimmel notes in a later work, "The Quran mentions only one woman by her actual name. This is Mary, the virgin mother of Jesus, who is highly revered in Islam. As one tradition has it, she will be the first to enter paradise. It was for her that the dried-up palm tree bore sweet dates as she clung to it during the labors of childbirth, and her newborn infant testified to her purity. She is the silent, humble soul who would deserve special and extensive study." Annemarie Schimmel, *My Soul Is a Woman: The Feminine in Islam* (Continuum, 1997), 55.

provided her with miracles and blessings. The chapter named after her in the Qur'an contains "one of the more dramatic and beloved discussions of a female figure in the Qur'an."[20] The story of Maryam would become a paradigm for later Sufis, especially women, who were drawn to her spiritual and mystical nature. Moreover, as discussed in the previous chapter, prophetic hadiths speak about Maryam as the "best woman" because her devotional acts give her special standing and reverence.

Sufis particularly celebrate the angelic touch that led to her pregnancy and the eventual birth of a righteous prophet and message-bearer. Thus, Maryam's "spiritual role of the female receptacle is fully accepted," and her pregnancy and birth are part of her divine struggle.[21] Unlike other Near Eastern philosophies, many Sufis held that motherhood and its various struggles, from pregnancy to labor, were part of a spiritual journey.[22] Maryam would thus become an exemplar "of the nature of the feminine ideal," which was further connected to the so-called feminine aspects of God, such as mercy (*rahma*).[23] The story of Maryam provides fodder for those of the mystical and Sufi persuasion, as her story is full of miracles, angels, and the divine.

---

20. Sells, *Early Islamic Mysticism*, 34.

21. Schimmel, *Mystical Dimensions of Islam*, 429. As Jamal Elias states, "Maryam, the immaculate virgin giving birth to the spirit-child Jesus, is a favorite of Muslim mystics. She is a perfect example of the human spirit being filled with divine light *(al-nur al-ilahi)* after receipt of divine inspiration. Her importance in Islamic spirituality is attested to by the number of Muslims who visit her shrine near Selpk (Ephesus) in Turkey, and by the pious references to her in mystical poetry." Jamal Elias, "The Female and Feminine in Islamic Mysticism," *Muslim World* 78 (1988): 209–224.

22. As Helminski further states, "Sufism also connects with the maternal or the 'womb' which carries and creates. Maryam embodies this spiritual womb as her maternal struggles are explained in detail in the Qur'an and with reverence." Helminski, *Women of Sufism*, xxvi.

23. Dakake, "Walking upon the Path of God Like Men?" 132.

## The Deputy of Maryam—Rabi'a al-'Adawiyya

Because of Maryam's spiritual role, she became a model for female saints and Sufis in general, who were drawn to her mystical and miraculous nature. Arguably the most famous female Muslim mystical figure is Rabi'a al-'Adawiyya (d. 185/801), frequently depicted in Maryam's light.[24] Rabi'a is described as the "one accepted by men,[25] as the second spotless Maryam."[26] Like Maryam, Rabi'a had no spouse and devoted herself to piety and worship.[27] She fits the model of a celibate women whose only care and concern are the love, grace, and mercy of God.[28] For instance, in the streets of Basra, she was asked why she was carrying

---

24. In her book *Rabi'a from Narrative to Myth*, Rkia Cornell tries to strike the balance between understanding Rabi'a as a mythical figure and one who continues to have cultural and religious significance. Rkia Cornell, *Rabi'a from Narrative to Myth: The Many Faces of Islam's Most Famous Woman Saint, Rabi'a al-'Adawiyya* (Oneworld Academic, 2019), 4. Nonetheless, she continues to explain that even though there is not strong historical data around her existence, her narrative and historical memory continue to be important. Similar things could be said about Maryam. Even though there is no strong historical data about Mary's life, her cultural and religious memory remains significant in two of the world's largest religions, Christianity and Islam. Understanding the different ways that Mary continues to motivate, inspire, and move people is one of the essential aspects of this book. Moreover, similar to Rabi'a, certain tropes of Maryam continue to be influential such as those of the celibate lover of God, religious teacher, ascetic, mystic, and icon. Maryam's presentation in both the Qur'an and hadith literature provides the framework, narratives, and tropes that continue throughout Islamic literature and influence how various righteous men and women are remembered and understood. These narratives and tropes further influence Muslim behavior and action today.

25. Dakake explains that Sufi women were frequently understood to be like "men, encompassing both male and female attributes." Dakake, "Walking upon the Path of God Like Men?" 138.

26. Merin Shobhana Xavier, "Gendering the Divine: Women, Femininity, and Queer Identities on the Sufi Path," *The Routledge Handbook of Islam and Gender*, ed. Justine Howe (Routledge, 2021), 166.

27. For an example of righteous and mystical women other than Rabi'a, see Arezou Azad, "Female Mystics in Mediaeval Islam: The Quiet Legacy," *Journal of the Economic and Social History of the Orient* 56 (2013): 53–88.

28. As Dakake explains, "However, the rejection of offers of marriage and male sexual attention—particularly from prominent male spiritual authorities—is a significant

a torch in one hand and a bucket of water in the other, and she famously said, "I want to throw fire into Paradise and pour water into Hell so that these two veils disappear, and it becomes clear who worships God out of love, not out of fear of Hell or hope for Paradise."[29]

Rabi'a is further described as "lost in love-union, deputy of Maryam, the pure, accepted among men, Rabi'a al-'Adawiyya—the mercy of God Most High upon her."[30] Here the author sees Rabi'a in the model of Maryam and even as her "deputy"; Rabi'a frequently fits the trope of a "teacher," specifically of older men who were religious authorities. Classical scholars saw that Rabi'a was one "endowed with reason and possessed the unique ability to conceptualize and express important truths."[31] Like other mystical women, Rabi'a was a "mentor" (*mu'addiba*) to men and part of a group of specialized teachers in the various Islamic sciences (*ustadh*), who had mixed audiences.[32] She was known to say words of wisdom or aphorisms "in which ethical and theological principles are expressed short, pithy sayings."[33] Each saying was meant to challenge the listener and push them to think in deeper and more spiritual terms. Her statements were not overly theoretical or abstract but built on a classical Islamic culture of teaching morals and practical wisdom.

Several stories narrate how Rabi'a was absorbed in the love of God and even accepted among men, similar to how Maryam was accepted by Zakariyya. For instance, just like Maryam taught Zakariyya a lesson regarding reliance on God by receiving fruits out of season, Rabi'a teaches the men around her spiritual lessons that were narrated and

---

theme in the Sufi literature pertaining to women"; Dakake, "Walking upon the Path of God Like Men?" 143.

29. Schimmel, *Mystical Dimensions of Islam*, 39, 429; Xavier, "Gendering the Divine: Women, Femininity, and Queer Identities on the Sufi Path," 166.

30. Sells, *Early Islamic Mysticism*, 155.

31. Cornell, *Early Sufi Women*, 56.

32. As Cornell notes, "The fact that such women transcended the social limitations of their femininity is revealed in as-Sulami's use of the masculine term *ustadh* when referring to their teaching roles." Cornell, *Early Sufi Women*, 59.

33. Cornell, *Early Sufi Women*, 56.

transmitted to others. For instance, a story is related about two religious dignitaries who came to pay their respects to her. Rabi'a served them two loaves of bread, but a beggar cried out, so she gave the bread to the one in need. The dignitaries were "dumbfounded," but immediately, a servant came in carrying warm loaves of bread. Rabi'a counted the loaves and found that there were eighteen. She said to the servant, "You've made a mistake" and told her, "Take them back."[34] The servant replied that there was nothing wrong, but Rabi'a insisted there was a mistake. The servant returned to her mistress, who added two more loaves and sent them back. Rabi'a counted and saw that there were now twenty and served them to her guests. They ate them and "marveled," asking, "What's the secret behind this?"[35]

Rabi'a explained that when she saw the two great men, she realized they were hungry and felt bad putting only two loaves in front of them. When the beggar came, she gave the loaves to him and prayed, "O my God, you have said, 'For each thing given, I will return ten-fold.' Certain of this, I have given away two loaves to please you, so that you would give back ten-fold." Based on this prayer, she knew that God would multiply by ten the two she had given and give her twenty. Thus, when the servant initially brought only eighteen loaves, Rabi'a knew there was a mistake.[36]

Like Maryam, Rabi'a teaches male religious authority figures (who were most likely older than her) a spiritual lesson in that God can multiply food and provisions and provide from unknown and hidden places. Rabi'a was confident in her prayer and had a deep trust in God (*tawakkul*), which is akin to that of Maryam. She knew that God could provide in unimaginable ways and had the power to multiply and reward her charity.[37]

---

34. Sells, *Early Islamic Mysticism*, 155.

35. Sells, *Early Islamic Mysticism*, 155.

36. Sells, *Early Islamic Mysticism*, 159.

37. Cornell explains that some early Sufis followed Mary's path of entrustment in God (*tawakkul*) and refused to earn a living because, like Mary, they depended on God to provide for all their needs. Cornell, *Early Sufi Women*, 154.

Again like Maryam teaching Zakariyya, Rabi'a also taught Sufyan al-Thawri (d. 161/778), a noted collector and disseminator of the Prophet Muhammad's traditions. According to reports, Rabi'a met Sufyan at the end of his life.[38] Similar to Zakariyya, who had given up hope of having a son and progeny, Sufyan was disillusioned about finding peace and security. While Zakariyya and Sufyan both spoke from the position of scholarship and religious authority, Maryam and Rabi'a instead spoke from direct experience of faith, spirituality, and mysticism.

For instance, in one story, Sufyan raises his hands and prays, "Oh God, grant me safety!" After he makes this prayer, Rabi'a weeps, leading him to ask her why she cries. She responds that he makes her weep, causing Sufyan to become defensive and ask how. She replies, "Have you not learned that true safety from the world is to abandon all that is in it? So how can you ask for such a thing while you are still soiled with the world?"[39] Similar to Maryam's lesson to Zakariyya, Rabi'a teaches Sufyan a spiritual lesson: To find safety in the world is to abandon it and not to give it more credence than it deserves. The safety that Sufyan so much desires is not in his physical surroundings but in his mental state, which provides the world with more than it warrants.[40]

Likewise, Rabi'a follows Maryam in the trope of an isolated woman imploring for God's help, solace, and mercy. As discussed in chapter 1, when Maryam was delivering 'Isa, she "withdrew to a distant place" (19:23). When the pains of labor became excruciating, she cried out, "'I wish I had been dead and forgotten long before all this!" (19:24). Nonetheless, a voice shared that a stream had been provided for her and that if she shook the palm tree, fresh dates would fall to her. Accordingly, God comforted Maryam in a time of isolated need and provided for her when things were unbearable and desperate. Similarly, when Rabi'a was on her way to Mecca for

38. Cornell, *Early Sufi Women*, 63.

39. Cornell, *Early Sufi Women*, 67.

40. Cornell, *Early Sufi Women*, 59.

the Hajj, she was left helpless in the desert for several days. She then cried out, "My God, I am sore at heart, Where will I go? I am a lump of earth, and that house is a rock. I must have you."[41] Here, Rab'ia emphasizes the love of God over that of the ritual of visiting the Ka'ba (the house of "rock") and circumambulating around it. God then responded directly to her, "Don't you see that when Moses—peace be upon him—desired a vision, we cast a few motes of self-manifestation upon the mountain and it shattered into forty pieces!"[42] While God does not answer Rabi'a's exact prayer, he nonetheless comforts her by speaking directly to her and explaining why he is not showing himself to her. The story also connects Rabi'a with the great prophet of Musa in a similar way to how Maryam is connected to Muhammad, Ibrahim, and 'Isa.

In a similar story, Rabi'a's donkey dies on her way to make pilgrimage to Mecca, leaving her stranded in the desert. After rejecting help from passersby, Rabi'a complains directly to God like a "dissatisfied wife that He has not provided for and protected her, a weak and helpless woman, on the journey to His house."[43] Instead of seeking the help of other people, Rabi'a speaks directly to the divine, her source of comfort and aid. Miraculously, the donkey comes back to life, similar to how 'Isa raises the dead in Qur'an 3:49, and she resumes her journey. In this story, God revives Rabi'a's resources rather than providing external support, similar to how Maryam is provided comfort through her surroundings and not by other people. The trope of the solitary woman who has a unique, intimate connection with God appears throughout Sufi literature.[44] By being alone, the pious protagonist is forced to return only to God, demonstrating their special and exclusive

41. Sells, *Early Islamic Mysticism*, 157.

42. Sells, *Early Islamic Mysticism*, 157.

43. Maria Dakake, "'Guest of the Inmost Heart': Conceptions of the Divine Beloved Among Early Sufi Women," *Journal of Comparative Islamic Studies* 3, no. 1 (2007): 75.

44. Dakake, "Guest of the Inmost Heart," 79.

relationship with the divine. In their call, they exhibit tremendous confidence and certainty that God will hear their appeal and respond to their concerns.[45]

Last, Rabiʿa is similar to Maryam in being an elect woman and one of the best of all time. As previously discussed, the Qur'an declares, "The angels said to Maryam: 'Mary, God has chosen you and made you pure: He has truly chosen you above all women'" (3:42). As stated in chapter 3, Muslim scholars understood this verse as referring to Maryam being one of the best women of all time, if not the best.[46] Likewise, classical Sufi scholars frequently included Rabiʿa as the only woman to merit a chapter in their books, demonstrating that she was "elected" and raised "above all the women of the world."[47] Like Maryam, Rabiʿa exemplified the characteristics of "chastity, divine election, and complete trust in God."[48] She was a unique woman who stood out among others and was noticed by various classical and modern scholars and historians.

## "Like Mary, We're Made Pregnant, Through That Touch"—Maryam in Mystical Poetry

Maryam's mystical import continues into mystical poetry, particularly that of the famous Sufi Rumi (d. 672/1273), whose poetry has a popular following throughout Muslim lands and even in Europe and North

45. As Dakake further states, "One of the most striking features of early female Sufi discourse is the tremendous confidence many of these women had both in God's love for them and in the rewards they could expect for their devotion to Him. While there are some examples of women weeping over their own moral unworthiness and their desire for God, it is at least as common to find Sufi women expressing certainty in their relationship with God, and a pronounced confidence that God has chosen them for His love, and that He loves them as they love Him." Dakake, "Guest of the Inmost Heart," 76.

46. See the previous chapter for a discussion.

47. Cornell, *Early Sufi Women*, 293.

48. Cornell, *Early Sufi Women*, 293.

America. Rumi was "above all he was a passionate lover of God who expressed his feelings in a poetically unorthodox, volcanic way, thus creating a style which is unique in the entire Persian literature."[49] His classic and most famous work is the *Masnavi*,[50] which has been translated into various languages and is divided into six books.[51] Some of the important themes in Rumi's poetry are "the importance of love to transcend attachments to the world . . . literal-mindedness and intellectualism."[52] After his death, his followers started the Mevlevi Sufi Order, which became famous for the whirling dervishes, a tradition that remains alive today in popular performances and mystical art. Rumi's poetry continues to be admired throughout Muslim-majority countries,

---

49. H. Ritter, "Djalal al-Din Rumi," in *Encyclopaedia of Islam, Second Edition*, ed. P. Bearman, Th. Bianquis, C. E. Bosworth, E. van Donzel, and W. P. Heinrichs (E. J. Brill, 2012).

50. A *mathnawi* is defined as "a poem based on independent, internally rhyming lines." J. T. P. de Bruijn, B. Flemming, and Munibur Rahman, "Matthnawi," in *Encyclopaedia of Islam*, 2nd ed., ed. P. Bearman, Th. Bianquis, C. E. Bosworth, E. van Donzel, and W. P. Heinrichs (E. J. Brill, 2012).

51. For more on Rumi's translations, see Omid Azadibougar and Simon Patton, "Coleman Barks' Versions of Rumi in the USA," *Translation and Literature* 24, no. 2 (2015): 172–189. Azadibougar and Patton criticize Bark's translations, namely because he does not know Persian and the historical context from which the poetry derived. Barks "Americanizes" Rumi, making him palatable to a Western audience rather than presenting his writings' Islamic and Eastern elements. Specifically, he presents sexual and physical love as connected to divine love and the poetry as entertaining rather than mystical and Sufi-related. This adaptation could lead to the problem of where "no traces of the original culture are left in the text," and the work is simply commercialized. Rather a "new" text has been created, which "functions in a field which has its own rules" and is disassociated from the original. Azadibougar and Patton contend that genuinely presenting Rumi as a reflection of his Islamic and Eastern context would better help in cross-cultural understanding rather than simply trying to Americanize him.

52. Jalaal al-Din Rumi, *The Masnavi, Book One* (Oxford University Press, 2004), xxvii. Also, M. Soileau notes that the main themes of the poetry "include the spiritual quest, the search for the inner significance of words and practices, the unity of existence, and especially divine love." Mark Soileau, "Rumi, Jalal al-Din," in *Encyclopedia of Islam*, ed. Juan E. Campo (Facts on File, 2009), 594.

especially in Turkey and Iran, and has become a "phenomenon" in the United States.[53] He is even considered a bridge builder between "Islam and the West" through forging a common spirituality between them and dissolving religious boundaries.[54] Nonetheless, while Rumi has been adopted into a new-age Sufism, which focuses on love and general spirituality, his poetry has a strong Islamic and Qur'anic influence, leading scholars to say that his poetry is a type of Qur'anic commentary (*tafsir*), as it demonstrates a deep understanding and appreciation of the text.[55] A true Sufi should internalize the Qur'an's message and "live and breathe

53. For instance, the book *Essential Rumi* has over 250,000 copies in print and "is easily the most successful poetry book published in the West in the past decade." Ptolemy Tompkins, "Rumi Rules!" *Time Magazine*, October 29, 2002. Moreover, "Coleman Barks, the translator whose work sparked an American Rumi renaissance and made Rumi the best-selling poet in the US, ticks off the reasons Rumi endures: 'His startling imaginative freshness. The deep longing that we feel coming through. His sense of humour. There's always a playfulness [mixed] in with the wisdom.'" Jane Ciabattari, "Why Is Rumi the Best-Selling Poet in the US?" *BBC Culture*, October 21, 2014. Nonetheless, Amira Zein expresses the critique that "for the time being, the popular (as opposed to the scholarly) perception of Rumi's Sufi tradition in the United States does not capture the perennial philosophy to which Rumi belongs. Instead, it brings a form of value spirituality entangled in relativity and temporality. Rumi's verse is seen as an enjoyable 'spiritual product' to be consumed in order that one may relax and become more productive after listening to it." Amira El-Zein, "Spiritual Consumption in the United States: The Rumi Phenomenon," *Islam Christian-Muslim Relations* 11, no. 1 (200): 83. El-Zein expresses the concern that Rumi is de-Islamicized to fit an American consumer market focused on loose, comfortable, and general spirituality. See also Elena Furlanetto, "The Rumi Phenomenon Between Orientalism and Cosmopolitanism: The Case of Elif Shafak's The Forty Rules of Love," *European Journal of English Studies* 17, no. 2 (2013): 201–213. Furlanetto contends that Rumi speaks to a post-9/11 readership that is searching for a counter to a "clash of civilization" model or one that seeks spiritual harmony between the "East" and the "West." Rumi challenges Islamophobia and presents a vision of Islam that is attractive to both American and Turkish readers, especially through Elif Shafak's *The Forty Rules of Love: A Novel of Rumi*.

54. Rumi, *The Essential Rumi*, trans. Coleman Barks (HarperOne, 2004), XVII.

55. El-Zein, "Spiritual Consumption in the United States," 81; Jalal al-Din Rumi and William Chittick, *The Sufi Path of Love: The Spiritual Teachings of Rumi* (State University of New York Press, 1983), 9.

in the words of the revelation."[56] Some have even labeled Rumi's poetry the "Persian Qur'an," not necessarily because it rivaled the scripture but because it translates it into an accessible medium and highlights the text's spiritual and moral messages.

When we examine Rumi's poetry, we see that he emphasizes certain spiritual themes explicitly related to Maryam, such as pregnancy, the divine path, and companionship. As he states:

With human souls the Absolute's connected—
From Him, rare pearls each human heart collected.
Like Mary, we're made pregnant, through that touch,
With the Messiah we adore so much!
Not the Messiah who walks in this place,
But that Messiah who's beyond all space.
The soul, once pregnant with the Holy One,
Then makes the whole world pregnant too, in turn.
Thus to a second world this world gives birth,
So resurrected souls see that world's worth.[57]

Here the spiritual journey is described through pregnancy. The soul is first touched and becomes "pregnant," which eventually leads to the world becoming "impregnated." Rumi makes this analogy to Maryam, who, in the Qur'an, is touched by the divine messenger angel Jibril, which leads her to become pregnant. The birth is not just of anybody but rather the Messiah, who "is beyond (the limitation of) measuring space." The Messiah would eventually change the world, but it all started with the first touch of the "soul," which became pregnant with divine blessings. The theme of pregnancy additionally appears with the "second

56. The full quote from Schimmel is "As a true Sufi should, have 'koranized' their memory and now live and breathe in the words of the revelation." El-Zein, "Spiritual Consumption in the United States," 81.

57. Jalal al-Din Rumi, *The Masnavi Book Two*, trans. J. A. Mojaddedi (Oxford University Press, 2007), 70.

world," or the day of judgment and resurrection. The world is pregnant with the dead and will give birth again in their resurrection. This line may allude to Qur'anic verses that describe the earth unloading its burdens on the day of resurrection or giving birth.[58] What is noteworthy here is Rumi's use of the metaphor of pregnancy, which is often associated only with women, in his discussions of spiritual transformation and growth.

The theme of pregnancy continues when Rumi presents the pregnant Maryam conversing with Elizabeth, the mother of John/Yahya the Baptist. Rumi prefaces this section by refuting the idea that humans need visible proof of the divine. He gives various examples, such as the fact that a thirsty person does not question the source of the water before they drink it or that when a mother calls her child to nurse, they do not question the origins of her milk. Rumi then makes an analogy between these examples and that of the Prophet, who, when "shouts out to dictate / Inwardly each of them bows down prostrate."[59] People naturally follow the Prophet's call—similar to that of a thirsty person and hungry child—because it speaks to something that is true, divine, and internal. This discussion of motherhood and prophecy leads Rumi to refer to an extra-Qur'anic story regarding Maryam's conversation with Elizabeth:

> John Baptist's mother secretly told Mary
> before she was delivered of her burden,
> "I saw there is a king in you for certain,
> a Lord of Constancy and wise apostle,
> Because when I came face to face with you
> my baby bowed to him, illustrious Lady!
> My fetus bowed in worship to your fetus—
> my body was in pain from bowing so."

58. Qur'an 99:2.

59. Rumi, *Book Two*, 211.

> And Mary said, "I also felt within me
> this baby's act of worship in my womb."[60]

The dialogue here is between mothers and how they experience their pregnancy and what resides in their womb. Elizabeth expresses that when she comes close to Maryam, she feels that her child, John/Yahya, bows down to her child, Jesus/'Isa, in a manner of respect and deference. Maryam does not directly respond to Elizabeth's feelings but rather expresses her own that her child also seems to be in a state of submission and worship. The story is significant because it has two pregnant mothers sharing their feelings about their unborn, which foreshadows the children's future relationship and how they will work together to spread their message.

In the next lines, Rumi chides skeptics who believe that this story is fictitious, as the Qur'an states that Maryam withdrew in her pregnancy and did not interact with anyone, such as Elizabeth. However, scholars note that for Rumi, "the story conveys a meaning and of how it can be read as a teaching rather than as a history."[61] As he later exclaims, "Just grasp the story's meaning, silly fool!"[62] Here, Rumi emphasizes the importance of meaning over historical accuracy and stresses that the reader should focus on the story's deeper and underlying significance rather than just its surface level. The one simply looking for historical facts is a "silly fool" who misses the greater purpose, lesson, and moral.

---

60. Alan Williams, "The Visitation of Mary and Rumi's Comments on the Nature of Story: 'Mathnawī,' Book Two," *Mawlana Rumi Review* 6 (2015): 119. Jawid Mojaddedi translates the section as the following: "John's mother spoke to Mary secretly, Before she gave birth of this mystery, 'I've seen that a great king is inside you, A prophet of God, who is steadfast too, When I encountered you by chance just now, The child inside my womb began to bow, My baby bowed to yours respectfully, And so I felt a strange new pang in me, 'Yes,' Mary said, 'In me a strange sensation, Told me about your embryo's prostration.'" Rumi, *Book Two*, 212.

61. Williams, "The Visitation of Mary," 119.

62. Williams, "The Visitation of Mary," 119.

Rumi further emphasizes spiritual communication and being able to see through the surface, or the "skin." As he states, "Those with true vision easily can view, Remote things as though they are present too." He further elaborates, "With eyes closed you can see your distant friend, if you can see through skin and comprehend."[63] These lines once again emphasize the deeper meaning of the story over the literal but also suggest that the babies, both John/Yahya and Jesus/'Isa, could sense and "see" one another through their mother's wombs. Even though their eyes had not developed and a womb separated them, they could still communicate and respond to each other. The same could be said of spiritual friendship and companionship in that true friends do not necessarily need words to communicate; they sense each other even across great distances and barriers.

Along with pregnancy, Rumi references Maryam when speaking about spiritual companionship, the soul, and its mirror image. Humans are mirrors to one another, seeking out people like themselves. As he exclaims, "This mirror for the soul is the saint's face, The one who is beyond all time and space, Heart, seek a mirror of this type! I'd scream, Reach for the ocean, and not a mere stream!"[64] Here, Rumi encourages his readers to reach for what is beyond and find spiritual company and guides that push one further. This leads Rumi to reference Maryam: "In this way, slaves reach God eventually: Pain led pure Mary to the date-palm tree." The pain of labor led Maryam to the palm tree, which she eventually shakes, and it provides comfort. Pain thus could be a means to find the divine and develop one's soul and internal mirror. Pain is not the antithesis of spiritual development but rather part of it. In other words, as scholars summarize, "The body is like Mary, and each of us has a Jesus within him. If the pain appears, our Jesus will be born. But if no pain comes, Jesus will return to his Origin on that same hidden road by which he came. We will be deprived of him and reap

63. Rumi, *Book Two*, 212.

64. Rumi, *Book Two*, 11.

no benefit."[65] Rumi, as a man, appears to identify with Maryam's labor pains even though he has never experienced them. He further emphasizes the "palm tree," which stresses the importance of solitude, prayer, and reflection. Maryam was alone when she experienced the pain but was eventually provided comfort by the same palm tree she withdrew to.

Last, Rumi emphasizes Maryam's relationship and encounter with the divine messenger as a metaphor for a spiritual friend and guide. As we recall, the Qur'an speaks about the "Spirit," which is understood to be angel Jibril, approaching Maryam and her feeling afraid of and resistant to him, even fearing his intentions. Rumi imagines this scene and Maryam's reaction because she was naked and taking a bath when the messenger approached her: "For she was naked and feared corruption."[66] Rumi describes the divine messenger as beautiful, causing her "exhilaration" and making her "heart pound." He continues,

> Like sun and moon, the spirit all can trust
> Rose up before her eyes from the ground's dust
> Beauty unveiled and rose up in this way
> Just as the sun appears each single day

For Rumi, the angel's beauty compared to the "sun and moon," which caused Maryam to "shiver" and be in a state of awe. He even makes an analogy between the messenger and the Prophet Yusuf, who is noted in the Qur'an for his handsomeness. However, for Rumi, Yusuf's beauty did not compare with the angel, and he would have "cut his hands," a reference to the Qur'anic story (12:31), if he had seen the messenger. Rumi then continues describing the spirit:

> Just like a rose in soil it magically
> Came up as if the heart's own fantasy

---

65. Chittick, *The Sufi Path of Love*, 241.

66. Jalal al-Din Rumi, *The Masnavi Book 3*, trans. J. A. Mojaddedi (Oxford University Press, 2013), 226.

She lost her wits as though she had just dreamed;
"I feel now to God's refuge!" she then screamed.

Here, Rumi reimagines the Qur'anic scene, not of one where Maryam fears the motives of an unwelcome intruder but rather one where Maryam is taken aback by the beauty of a divine messenger. The young Maryam is unable to think or feel, which causes her to seek refuge. As Rumi exclaims, "She'd seen some amorous glances which could start / Fires to burn intellects and pierce men's hearts."[67] Maryam feels anxious and agitated, "like fish on land who had been relocated." Just like a fish feels discomfort when transported to the land, Maryam feels anxiety and apprehension at the appearance of the unknown messenger. Rumi points out that one may initially reject the divine messenger and their beauty because one doesn't fathom their true meaning and depth.

After describing Maryam's concern and agitation, Rumi pictures the messenger's response to her reluctance, fear, and nervousness:

Generous God's representative then said:

"I come from Him. Trust me and don't feel dread.
Don't turn your gaze from God's exalted ones.
Don't draw back from His special confidants."
As he said this, a ray of purest light
Rose out of his lips up to the stars' height.
"To nothingness would you flee my existence?
I'm like a king beyond in Non-existence.
My origin and home are in Non-Being;
My form in front of Mary's all you're seeing.
I am difficult form now to view—
I'm the new moon and the heart's image too.
You cannot flee an image in your heart;
It goes with you wherever you depart.
But not the worthless transient fancies—they,
Just like a false dawn, quickly fade away

67. Rumi, *Book 3*, 226.

I'm like the true dawn, made out of God's light,
Whose day will never be replaced by night.
Mary, don't cry out 'God's strength!' out of fear,
Since from God's strength I have descended here
And its's my sustenance and origin:
God's strength's light shone before speech could begin.
You seek out refuge now in God from me,
But I've been there since Pre-eternity.
"I am that refuge. I've saved you so often
Now you seek refuge and must have forgotten."
Failure to recognize is the worst thing:
In her arms, but unskilled in love-making
You think your friend's the stranger, and you want
To name joy "grief"; you're truly ignorant.[68]

The messenger here seems to be taken aback and almost offended that Maryam does not recognize him. He starts off by stating, "I come from Him. Trust me and don't feel dread." He wants Maryam not to be scared of him but rather recognize and appreciate his existence and message. In particular, he seems hurt by Maryam's Qur'anic statement, "I truly seek refuge in the Most Compassionate from you! So leave me alone if you are God-fearing" (19:18). The messenger originates from God, which is the reason why he descended to Maryam in the first place. He is "that refuge" that Maryam seeks, as he has "saved [her] so often." While Maryam didn't initially realize it, he was the messenger who had been there all along, guiding her actions and supporting her when in need.

Rumi further emphasizes the beauty of the messenger, something that is not explicit in the Qur'an. For Rumi, the messenger is made of "purest light," and when he spoke, light "rose out of his lips up to the stars' height." The messenger is like a true moon, which represents the "true dawn, made out of God's light / Whose day will never be replaced by night." The messenger is and brings light that originates from the divine. This light will not set like the sun, and there will be no "night"

68. Rumi, *Book 3*, 230.

or spiritual darkness. The messenger urges Maryam to accept the light and guidance, even though she initially does not recognize it and is afraid of what it could mean.

What is also striking is that Rumi does not mention 'Isa at all but rather focuses on the relationship between the messenger and Maryam. Maryam is initially fearful, agitated, and worried, but the messenger seeks to comfort her, explaining that he comes from the divine and represents God's beauty, guidance, and light. Here, Rumi does not emphasize Maryam's role as mother whatsoever but rather emphasizes the importance of recognizing the divine messenger when he appears and following his actions and calls. As Rumi states, "Failure to recognize is the worst thing," as acknowledgment is the first step toward submission, assistance, and love. Before 'Isa can appear, Maryam must accept the messenger and the message he brings.

## Conclusion

From Rabi'a to Rumi, Maryam provided a template for divine seekers to pursue God in Qur'anic and prophetic ways. Maryam presents a model who teaches those around her the spiritual lessons of daily life. She inspires celibate ascetics whose only concern is the love of God and returning to the divine. She makes us reflect on "pregnancy" and how all believers are "pregnant" with divine favors, blessings, and light. She inspires us to think more deeply regarding concepts of spiritual companionship and accepting the divine messengers when they appear. In contrast to the other disciplines, Sufism and mysticism focus on the aspects of Maryam related to the believer's spiritual journey and connect us to issues relating to God's blessings, deliverance, and miracles.

CHAPTER FIVE

# Maryam in Islamic Art and Film

WE HAVE DISCUSSED Maryam in several contexts, ranging from the sacred texts of Islam to her role in theology and mysticism. In this chapter, we explore how these texts, stories, and traditions have manifested in Islamic art and film. Whether it is through passages from the Qur'an or her respected role as a female mystic, we survey how artists have imagined Maryam and depicted her story. Through Islamic art and film, we experience a new commentary on Maryam that supplements and builds on the textual tradition.

## Defining Islamic Art

Islamic art has been defined as "the art made by artists or artisans whose religion was Islam, for patrons who lived in predominantly Muslim lands, or for purposes that are restricted or peculiar to a Muslim population or a Muslim setting."[1] The lands of Islam not only encompass "the arid belt covering much of West Africa but stretching from the Atlantic coast of North Africa and Spain on the west to the steppes of Central Asia and the Indian Ocean on the east."[2] While Islamic art has

---

1. Sheila S. Blair and Jonathan M. Bloom, "The Mirage of Islamic Art: Reflections on the Study of an Unwieldy Field," *Art Bulletin* 85, no. 1 (2003): 152–184. I agree with Blair and Bloom that Islamic art should not be confined to certain geographic and national lines but rather be an open discipline and humanistic in its nature. Depictions of Maryam can help us better understand not only Muslim and Islamic religion and culture but also religion and human society. It could also be said that "Islamic art" has also been created by both non-Muslims and Muslim minorities.

2. Blair and Bloom, "The Mirage of Islamic Art," 152.

frequently been defined as any art produced in these regions, the interest of this chapter is to examine Islamic art as religiously and spiritually motivated art, akin to Christian art. Specifically, Muslim depictions of Maryam represented their understanding of how scripture manifested within their imaginations. Maryam has been depicted throughout time and space, and her depictions are both similar and different throughout various contexts and geographical locations.

Nonetheless, before we start our discussion of Maryam, we first must deal with challenges in how we understand Islamic art and particularly the dominant perception of the "Islamic prohibition of the image." From the very beginning of its history, "the Islamic world replaced representations with written formulae" and therefore transformed "the image into the word," making representations less prominent.[3] This "transformation" was influenced by Christian and Byzantine art, as the burgeoning Islamic Empire built on those before it. Instead of simply destroying images of previous civilizations, Muslims and Muslim rulers eventually "replaced" them with the written word in Islamic spaces, often from selected passages of the Qur'an.[4]

Instead of thinking of a "prohibition" of images, it is better to think of Islam endorsing aniconism, or shying away from images.[5] We could succinctly state that it is incorrect to "talk of a Muslim iconoclasm, even if destruction of images did occur later; one should rather call

3. Oleg Grabar, "From the Icon to Aniconism: Islam and the Image," *Museum International* 218, no. 55 (2003): 51. See also Oleg Grabar, ed., "Islamic Attitudes Towards Arts," in *The Formation of Islamic Art* (Yale University Press, 1987); G. S. Hodgson, "Islam and Image," *History of Religions* 3, no. 2 (1964): 220–260; Fariha Ali, "Aniconism in Islam," *al-Salihat* 1, no. 2 (2022): 1–16.

4. Taha Jaber al-Alwani, "'Fatwa' Concerning the United States Supreme Courtroom Frieze," *Journal of Law and Religion* 15, no. 1/2 (2000–2001): 1–28.

5. Terry Allen, "Aniconism and Figural Representation in Islamic Art," in *Five Essays on Islamic Art* (Solipsist Press, 1988), 17–37. Allen explains that Islamic culture left "artistic narrative to speech" rather than displaying it in pictures.

the Muslim attitude aniconic."[6] As discussed in chapter 2, the Prophet Muhammad is reported to have removed images from the Ka'ba, creating a precedent that Muslim houses of worship would be free of images and icons. However, this does not mean that Islam is devoid of depictions, which still appear in books, houses, courts, and palaces.[7] Moreover, artists were more amenable to depicting Maryam because there was no consensus that she was a prophet,[8] allowing her to be portrayed while other prophetic figures were not. For the fear of polytheism, Islamic prophets were not always depicted, as they could eventually be worshipped alongside God, as previous communities had done.[9]

The question of iconoclasm is further important to Qur'anic and biblical figures as Ibrahim is the only figure in the Qur'an who is an "iconoclast," or breaks images (21:51-70). As a rebellious youth, Abraham questions his dad's making of idols and then smashes the town's "gods" except for the biggest one. Various Qur'anic exegetes from classical to modern times did not see this act as against all images but only those worshipped, or "idols."[10] The story thus affirms *tawhid* or absolute monotheism rather than a blanket prohibition against all images.[11]

---

6. Richard Ettinghausen, Sheila Blair, and Oleg Grabar, *The Art and Architecture of Islam, 650–1250* (Yale University Press, 1994), 6. See also Oleg Grabar, "Islam and Iconoclasm," in *Early Islamic Art, 650–1100, volume I, Constructing the Study of Islamic Art* (Ashgate, 2005), 45–56.

7. For a larger discussion of the Prophet Muhammad being depicted within the US Supreme Court, see Al-Alwani, "'Fatwa' Concerning the United States Supreme Courtroom Frieze," 28.

8. See chapter 3 for discussions of her prophecy.

9. Islam, for instance, saw Jesus/'Isa as a prophet and rejected him as the son of God. Theologians continued to be concerned that other prophets could be worshipped alongside God and made to associate with God.

10. Younus Y. Mirza, "Abraham as an Iconoclast," *Islam and Christian–Muslim Relations* 16, no. 4 (2005): 413–428.

11. To see how this story fits within contemporary Muslim iconoclasm, see Barry Finbar Flood, "Idol-Breaking as Image-Making in the 'Islamic State,'" *Religion and Society: Advances in Research* 7 (2016): 116–138.

The academic study of Islamic art has further been critiqued for focusing only on the secular aspects of the art and not probing into its "religious motivation."[12] The field of art history has frequently exhibited a "disciplinary aversion to religious models for understanding the art of the Islamic world."[13] While key art historians have contributed to various fields and subdisciplines, they often overlook the spiritual, religious, and textual impulses for such work.[14] It is important to note that "Islam needs to be considered as an important intellectual source of meaning for artist and audience alike."[15] Specifically, there is a frequent lack of appreciation for how the Qur'an and its subsequent interpretative tradition shaped Islamic art.[16] This observation is essential when we examine the depictions of Maryam, which are often contextualized within a historical period rather than analyzed in terms of how they relate to the Qur'an and the later interpretative tradition.[17]

---

12. Moya Carey and Margaret S. Graves, "Introduction: The Historiography of Islamic Art and Architecture, 2012," *Journal of Art Historiography* 6 (2012): 1–15. See also Emel Esin, "The Qur'anic Verses and the Hadith as Sources of Inspiration in Islamic Art," in *Islamic Art: Common Principles, Forms and Themes*, ed. Ahmad Muhammad 'Isa and Tahsim Omer Tahaoglu (Dar al-Fikr, 1989), 73–83.

13. Carey and Graves, "Introduction: The Historiography of Islamic Art," 14. While I draw on Islamic art history in this chapter, I am compelled to write on the religious motivation of Maryam, which is driven from the previous chapters.

14. Robert Hillenbrand, "Oleg Grabar: The Scholarly Legacy," *Journal of Art Historiography* no. 6 (2012): 1–35. As Hillenbrand explains, Grabar "did not make it a high priority to probe in depth the religious impulse in Islamic art" (13).

15. Wendy Shaw, "The Islam in Islamic Art History: Secularism and Public Discourse," *Journal of Art Historiography* 6 (2012): 1–34, at 33. I agree with Shaw's general argument in using the term "Islamic art" but also see the challenges of using the term regarding scope and meaning.

16. Hillenbrand, "Oleg Grabar," 14. He explains, "But above all, [Grabar] never grappled in full detail with the many-layered impact of the Qur'an on Islamic art and the people who produced it."

17. Isma'il al-Faruqi, *The Arts of Islamic Civilization* (International Institute of Islamic Thought, 2013). Al-Faruqi ends his article by stating, "The Islamic Arts therefore can rightfully be designated 'Qur'anic arts.'" See also Isma'il R. al-Faruqi, "Islam and Art," *Studia Islamica* 37 (1973): 81–109.

Last, it is essential to look at the politics of Islamic art where it often exists (in museums) and before the advent of modernity, or the 1800s. After that, European models of art dominate, and Islamic art may no longer exist in the minds of historians. Islam and Islamic art are seen as "static," not evolving or at the same level as European and Enlightenment art.[18] This contrast between modern Western art and classical Islamic art is connected to attempts to create a "moderate Islam" that is distinct and different from "conservative" and "fundamentalist" movements. "Good Muslims" are understood to produce art and culture while living in the past. In contrast, "bad Muslims" shun art, destroy icons, and live in the present.[19] Islamic art thus takes on a new dimension in terms of global politics, where certain types of art represent an ideal Islam, which powerful nations and governments want Muslims to be.

Depictions of Maryam can help portray positive representations of Islam and bring together various religious communities. Nonetheless, we should be careful not to use her to divide and subjugate various Muslim communities but rather to better understand the complex and dynamic Islamic interpretative tradition.

## Maryam in Classical Islamic Art

The various classical depictions of Maryam focus on two major themes: her encounter with Jibril and the birth of 'Isa. It is fascinating to note that the various scenes do not depict Maryam's own annunciation or her mother's concern in giving birth to a boy. Nor do they capture Maryam's

18. Shaw, "The Islam in Islamic Art History," 25. As she states, "If, as is suggested in both Orientalist and revivalist definitions of Islam, this Islam is defined as inherently corrupt, excluded from 'proper' Islam, then there can indeed be no properly 'Islamic' art."

19. Finbarr Barry Flood, "From Prophet to Postmodernism? New World Orders and the End of Islamic Art," in *Making Art History: A Changing Discipline and Its Institutions*, ed. Elizabeth Mansfield (Routledge, 2007), 31–53. Flood argues that Western museums often see themselves preserving a tolerant and enlightened Muslim past that can be "rejuvenated" to create an Islamic modernity.

dialogue with Zakariyya regarding the fruits or Maryam's return to her people and the baby Jesus's defense of her. Instead, Islamic artists were drawn to the moment the angel spoke to her, representing the moment of divine communication and touch. The angel Jibril appearing before her was unique within the prophet stories, as many others do not have such close and intimate divine access. Additionally, artists were inspired by the birth of 'Isa as the story's climax and the beginning of a new prophet.

Maryam appears in several places in art produced under the Ayyubid dynasty, built by Salah al-Din b. Ayyub (d. 589/1193) after he defeated the Crusaders and took over the lands of Egypt, Jerusalem, and Syria. Yet, even with the Ayyubids' repulsion of the Crusaders, the "mutual influence between Christian art and Islamic art was present throughout ages with various concentrations,"[20] with direct contact between the Ayyubids and Christians persisting through war, peace treaties, and trade. For instance, Ayyubid art depicts Maryam through carvings within incense burners, large plates, candlesticks, and canteens. Most of the metal pieces were made by Muslims, but Christian minorities most likely created some, as they emphasize themes like the crucifixion.[21]

The various themes of the art range from the annunciation to 'Isa's birth and baptism. For instance, the annunciation scene is depicted in one engraving on a basin, in which the angel Jibril approaches Maryam and informs her that she will give birth. A winged Jibril reaches out his hand, almost touching Maryam from behind, representing their divine connection and link. Maryam is shown turning around and appears to be surprised, startled, and even scared by the stranger's presence. The scene nicely captures the Qur'anic scene in the chapter of Maryam

20. Heba Mahmoud Saad Abdel Naby and Heba Magdy, "The Representation of Virgin Mary in Islamic Art During the Ayyubid Dynasty (12th–13th Century)," *International Journal of History and Cultural Studies* (*IJHCS*) 4, no. 4 (2018): 20.

21. However, it is possible that Muslim artists could have created crucifix scenes for a Christian market.

where she is by herself and first seeks refuge from the divine creature who appears as a man. The various images of Mary are thus influenced by both Christian and Islamic themes and represent the diverse context of the Ayyubid dynasty.

Persian and Ottoman art frequently depicts Maryam in the genre of the "Stories of the Prophet" (*Qisas al-Anbiya'*) and the Falnama (Book of Omens). In one painting from a sixteenth-century Falnama manuscript, Maryam is nursing her son while he offers her sustenance, potentially the dates mentioned in the Qur'anic chapter of Maryam. The picture suggests that 'Isa was the voice "which cried out from below" and told her to drink from the stream and shake the palm tree. In the painting, they are nourishing each other, demonstrating their deep connection, care, and concern for one another. Both figures have a halo and light above and around their heads, which signals that they are prophetic and divinely blessed figures. Nonetheless, Maryam towers over her child in a blue scarf and has features that make her appear Asian such as a small nose and wide eyes. She is the focus of the painting, with her body and face larger than anyone else's. There is no doubt Maryam is the protagonist, which is consistent with her portrayal in the Qur'anic narratives and prophetic reports. In contrast, 'Isa is depicted as an infant, not as a young child, which is closer to how he is described in the Qur'anic story. He is dwarfed by his mother but still visible and prominent in her lap. A figure, potentially the angel Jibril, is visible in the background, over the mountain range, and on the far right. The figure appears to be looking over Maryam and 'Isa, representing that divine and celestial beings watch over them as they grow and nourish one another. Even though they remain on earth, they are still under the care and concern of God, demonstrating that their actions are providential. The scene is set in an almost heavenlike garden with beautiful flowers, rocks, and greenery. The garden presents the forthcoming abode of Maryam and 'Isa in that their future will be together in heaven.

Mughal art originates from what is known as modern India and often links "the articulation of Mughal ancestry, the dynasty's imperial ideology through the female line, and the images' relationship to European paintings and prints."[22] One of the foundational rulers of the Mughal Empire, Akbar (r. 1556–1605), promoted a policy of *sulh-i kull*, or "peace with all," to his diverse population, which included Muslims, Hindus, and Christians.[23]

Maryam had a part to play in the Mughal dynasty's self-understanding. Akbar's mother was called by the honorific Maryam Makani, or "she who is equal to Maryam in rank," while Akbar's wife and Emperor Jahangir's mother was called Maryam Zamani, or "Mary of her Age." The court historian compared Maryam to the mother of Alanqoa, who was the Mughal dynasty's legendary ancestor and was believed to have been impregnated with divine light. The historian makes an analogy between the two women by stating that Alanqoa was resting in bed when suddenly a magnificent light shed its rays into her tent. The light eventually entered her mouth, and she became pregnant, just like Maryam, the daughter of 'Imran. Thus, the mother of the Mughal dynasty, Alanqoa, is understood similarly to Maryam in that God inspired the birth of her children. The lineage of Alanqoa, such as Akbar, is seen like 'Isa, who was a prophet with a divine mission. The court historian explains, "If you listen to tales of Maryam, then incline likewise to Alanqoa." By comparing Alanqoa to Maryam, the historian "bolsters" the political and spiritual legitimacy of Akbar and the Mughal Empire, arguing that they possess divine light and blessings.

Scholars link the proliferation of images of Maryam in the Mughal dynasty with the gifts of Jesuits to the emperors and the interaction of local artists with Renaissance art that the royal elite collected. For instance, in 1580, Jesuits noted that the emperor "had pictures of Christ, Mary, Moses and Muhammad."[24] The emperors

---

22. Mika Natif, "Images of the Virgin Mary in Mughal Art," *Khamseen: Islamic Art History Online*, March 28, 2024.

23. Mika Natif, *Mughal Occidentalism: Artistic Encounters Between Europe and Asia at the Courts of India, 1580–1630* (Brill 2018), 27.

24. Natif, "Images of the Virgin Mary in Mughal Art," Khamseen Islamic Art History Online, accessed April 24, 2025, https://sites.lsa.umich.edu/khamseen/topics/2024/images-of-the-virgin-mary-in-mughal-art/.

thus had a "multi-confessional mindset" where different art pieces influenced each other. One image reproduces the famous Salus Populi Romani from the church of the Santa Maria Maggiore in Rome. Because of their belief in divine powers, Christians replicated the image and disseminated it throughout the world, many times as an attempt to convert local populations to Catholicism. In the Mughal reproduction, the artists removed the child's hand gesture, which was related to the Christian benediction of raising the index and middle finger. Instead, the Mughal picture depicts Jesus as a toddler, according to the Qur'anic story where 'Isa is presented only as an infant, not a young child. The painting focuses more on Maryam, who "towers over" her child, creating a "strong sense of her presence." Maryam is looking away from 'Isa but still embracing him in her lap with both hands. The emphasis on Maryam reinforces the Mughal understanding of her as a spiritual matriarch with a birth story similar to that of Alanqoa.

In another painting, Akbar's son and successor, Jahangir, holds a picture of the Virgin Mary that "manifests ideas of ancestral veneration, genealogy and legitimacy through Mary."[25] Jahangir (r. 1605–27) is dressed in his royal garb of a red turban and pearl necklace and is shown gazing at a painting solely of Maryam, who is shown from the waist up and looking down. Through the picture, the ruler creates a "direct link" between himself and the divinely chosen Maryam. Around his head is a halo reminiscent of paintings of Islamic prophets who often are associated with light and divine guidance. In the painting, Maryam "is no longer the mother of God, but one of the matriarchs of the illustrious Mughal dynasty."[26] Maryam's image enhances the legitimacy and power of the Mughal Empire through a figure revered in Islamic tradition and European Christianity.

This painting was possibly made as a counterpart to another of Jahangir holding a picture of his father, Akbar. In the picture, Akbar is aged (looking fatherly), haloed, and holding an orb as a symbol of

25. Natif, "Images of the Virgin Mary in Mughal Art."

26. Natif, "Images of the Virgin Mary in Mughal Art."

sovereignty. In contrast, Jahangir looks younger, regal in royal garb, and prominent in front of a black background. Similar to the first picture, Jahangir is holding the picture, this time of his father, and gazing at it with reverence and respect. The two paintings taken together demonstrate how the Mughal Empire created legitimacy through both "the historical and mythological,"[27] with Jahangir taking spiritual and religious legitimacy from Maryam and ancestral and ruling legitimacy from Akbar.

Through Maryam, the Mughals were able to create a narrative on the choosiness of their rulers and connect with local spirituality and European Christianity. The various images of Maryam within Akbar's and Jahangir's times demonstrate how Mughals highlighted females within their spiritual lineage, drew from Renaissance art, and competed with Europeans for power and prestige. The emphasis on Maryam would lead to other Mughal paintings focusing on women as the subject matter.

## Film: *The Message*

Modern feature films also incorporate Maryam, especially films on the life and legacy of the Prophet Muhammad. As discussed above, Muslims have debated the portrayal of images and icons throughout their history and come to different conclusions in different geographies, situations, and contexts. Nonetheless, Muslims began to accept film in the modern age, as it was seen as a "sign" and "shadow" reinforcing God's power rather than competing against it.[28] Like other modern religious followers, Muslims saw film's power and influence on global audiences and as a medium to spread their message and values. Films

27. Natif, "Images of the Virgin Mary in Mughal Art."

28. Freek L. Bakker, "The Image of Muhammad in *The Message*, the First and Only Feature Film About the Prophet of Islam," *Islam and Christian–Muslim Relations* 17, no. 1 (2006): 78. For discussions of the permissibility of cinema in Iran and Shi'ism, see Nacim Pak-Shiraz, *Shi'i Islam in Iranian Cinema: Religion and Spirituality in Film* (I. B. Tauris 2011).

on Moses and Jesus began to appear in the second half of the twentieth century, leading Muslims to do the same regarding Muhammad.[29]

The 1976 film *The Message* is arguably the most important twentieth-century cinematic depiction of the life and legacy of the Prophet Muhammad.[30] The director struggled with Islamic aniconism and chose not to depict Muhammad, even though his camel and walking stick are sometimes portrayed. At times, the camera takes the place of Muhammad with the audience seeing from the Prophet's point of view. Like Muhammad, Maryam is not visually depicted in the film. However, her memory remains alive in the poignant scene where Muslims use her as a bridge figure with the Christian king of Abyssinia, the Negus.[31]

In this dramatic scene, the Quraysh envoy attempts to retrieve the Muslims from Abyssinia from the Christian king Negus, emphasizing that the Muslims are rebels. After several exchanges, the debate centers on Jesus, with the Negus asking the Muslims to relate what they believe about him. The Muslims, led by Ja'far b. Talib, explain that "God cast his holy spirit into the womb of a virgin named Mary" and that she "conceived Christ, the Apostle of God." The leader of the Quraysh, 'Amr b. al-'As, retorts that they believe that Jesus is an "apostle," not the "son of God." The Negus then demands that Ja'far relate what the Muslims' "miracle" or the Qur'an says about the "birth of our dear Lord Jesus Christ." Ja'far requests that he recite from the Qur'an, and the Negus agrees and asks him to come closer to him. While staring at 'Amr, Ja'far takes several steps toward the Negus, fixes his gaze on him, and recites verses 16–18 from the chapter of Maryam: "Relate in the book, the story of Mary. How she withdrew from her family to a place in the East. How we sent to her our angel, Gabriel, who said, 'I am a messenger from your God, to announce the birth of a holy Son to you.' She said, 'How shall I, Mary, have a son when no man has touched me?' And

29. These films included *The Ten Commandments* and *Jesus Christ Superstar*.

30. Moustafa Akkad, dir., *The Message* (Trancas, 1976).

31. See chapter 2 for more on this encounter.

Gabriel replied, 'For your Lord says it will happen. We appoint him a sign unto man and mercy from us. It is a thing ordained.'" While Ja'far recites the verses, peaceful and calm music plays in the background, emphasizing the recitation and Qur'anic miracle. The camera moves to capture the different faces while Ja'far recites: The bishops nod their heads and begin to tear up; the followers of the Negus intensely listen to the revelation and try to understand its meaning; and 'Amr and his associates frown, acknowledging that the Qur'an is divine and that they are losing their argument.

After finishing the recitation, Ja'far looks up, and the camera moves back to the Negus, who is visibly moved. After collecting himself, he takes several steps toward Ja'far to the point that they are face to face and declares, "The difference between us and you is not bigger than this line." As he makes this pronouncement, he draws a line between Ja'far and himself with his staff, which has a large gold cross on it. He then turns to 'Amr and declares, "Not for a mountain of gold will I give them up to you!" He turns to Ja'far and states, "You may live in Abyssinia in peace for as long as you wish. May God's blessings be upon you." The Muslims begin to celebrate by hugging one another, and Ja'far looks at the Negus with joy, appreciation, and gratitude.

It is important to note that no depiction of Maryam is made in the scene or the film in general. Instead, the Qur'an speaks about her and describes her plight and story. Through the story of the Negus and Maryam, the film thus tries to positively present Christians as hospitable and open to Muslims. It further attempts to appeal to Christian audiences who would appreciate positive portrayals of Jesus and Christian rulers.[32]

When we compare the scene to that found in the biography of Muhammad by Ibn Hisham (discussed in chapter 2), we see some notable differences. As we may recall, in Ibn Hisham's text, Umm Salama narrates the encounter with Negus, which is full of emotion, fear, and trepidation. The director likely chose not to depict Umm Salama because she became one of the wives of the Prophet Muhammad,

32. Bakker, "The Image of Muhammad in *The Message*," 80.

and they used similar standards as with Muhammad.[33] Nonetheless, it is clear that Umm Salama's narration influences the director's portrayal, capturing the deep emotion, drama, and tension that existed between the Quraysh and the early Muslim community as it centered on the Negus and Abyssinia. However, the director is keen to make Maryam and Christ the center of the encounter with Negus and the key reasons why he agrees to have them stay. While Ja'far speaks about the Muslim creed and the corruption of Arabian society in general, the scene climaxes on the recitation of the chapter of Maryam and the birth of Christ. Moreover, Ibn Hisham records that some bishops objected to the Negus's words, especially the idea that the difference between the Muslims and themselves was the line of a stick. However, in the film, the bishops seem to agree with the Negus and do not present any opposition to his statements or his desire to have the Muslims live peacefully in the land. Thus, the film strikes an even more ecumenical tone than found within the biographical literature, with the Abyssinian Christians welcoming the Muslims in unison.[34]

---

33. In fact, none of the wives of the Prophet Muhammad is depicted or even mentioned, other than Khadija, which may create the image that Muhammad was a celibate figure like that of Jesus and the Buddha. Bakker, "The Image of Muhammad in *The Message*," 87.

34. Moreover, when the English version of *The Message* is compared to the Arabic one, we see that the storyline is identical, but there are some distinctions in terms of language and presentation. The Arabic version is not simply dubbed from the English one but has different actors and scripts that follow the English one but also differ. For instance, when Negus asks the Muslims why they have come to Abyssinia, Ja'far says that they have come because Abyssinians are from "the People of the Book" (*ahl-kitab*), a Qur'anic phrase that speaks of both Jews and Christians as being people of scripture. When the discussion centers on Jesus and his role, they state that "we don't differentiate between any of the messengers." Once again, a Qur'anic reference speaks to the idea that all of the prophets are from God and that Muhammad was simply in the line of messengers. Moreover, when Negus asks Ja'far about the birth of Christ, he recites from the Qur'an in its original and rhyming form, which seems to have a larger impact than the English translation, as the bishops and Negus not only tear up but also begin to cry. The Arabic version therefore uses key Qur'anic phrases to show the similarity and affinity between Islam and Christianity. It further emphasizes the Qur'an, and the chapter of Maryam in particular, as a miracle, as it has a profound

## *Maryam the Saint*

While *The Message* intentionally does not depict prophetic figures, *Maryam the Saint* (Maryam Moghadas), produced by the Iranian film industry, takes an alternative approach.[35] The film uses Maryam's story to advance notions of women's leadership, challenge notions of the religious elite, and emphasize miracles and the unseen. However, one of the main challenges of creating successful religious epics is maintaining the balance between religious and historical authenticity and dramatic effect.[36] Specifically, the centrality of the Qur'an is essential to producing religious authenticity, and developing captivating, engaging, and appealing characters is necessary to attract audiences.

The film begins with the king waking from a dream that the arrival of the Messiah is imminent, which startles the guards. He then runs to the roof, crying in agony and fearing the loss of his power. A group of Jews has approached the palace, hoping that the Messiah has appeared and that the "humiliation of the Jews will end tonight." Some of them mention the news of a baby about to be born who could be the potential savior. The high priests nonetheless refute the claims, declaring that none of the signs of the Messiah has appeared and that they will inform the people when the necessary signs are apparent. Zakariyya is then shown entering the birthing room, which is full of solace, anger, and frustration. He speaks to Anna/Hana, who explains that she had a girl rather than a boy. One of the women in her company exclaims, "The birth of a girl is a disgrace to any family!" They begin to discuss what they should do next, with the idea emerging that the family should stay indoors until the "scandal" and "disgrace" pass. Zakariyya

---

effect on its listeners and allows the Muslims to stay in Abyssinia. The Arabic version continues the ecumenical tone of the English ones but stresses the Qur'an and Qur'anic phrases as a bridge between the two religions.

35. Shahriar Bahrani, dir., *Maryam Moghaddas* (Sima Film WN Media, 2000).

36. Nacim Pak-Shiraz, "The Qur'anic Epic in Iranian Cinema," *Journal of Film and Religion* 20, no. 1 (2015): 1–27. See also her book *Shi'i Islam in Iranian Cinema: Religion and Spirituality in Film.*

intervenes and states, "Do you find fault in the mercy of God?" He then demands the people to go away until he is alone with Hana and then asks whether the child is healthy, to which Hana responds yes. The scene demonstrates that while the townspeople reject Maryam because she is a female, Zakariyya accepts her and wants her to have a healthy upbringing.

The scene transitions back to the palace, where the king and advisers are discussing what they should do with the arrival of the Messiah. However, they soon realize that the so-called Messiah is a girl and that they have no reason to worry about losing their power. The king even mocks the idea and jokes, "I never thought my successor would be a girl!" The king's inner circle laughs hysterically at such an absurd suggestion. The film thus captures the Qur'anic discussion around the birth of Maryam and girls in general and how they were often neglected in pre-Islamic societies.

The film returns to Hana, who begins to talk to God under the full moon and night stars, holding her baby, Maryam. She thanks God for "this blessing" but explains her vow was for her child to serve the temple, but God gave her a girl. God knows how much she loves her child, but she will maintain her vow and put her child in the service of God. The townspeople have banished her and left her alone, and she doesn't know if the priests will accept her female child. Hana announces she has named her child "Maryam, your servant." The scene returns to showing the stars, suggesting that the divine gaze is watching over Hana and Maryam.

However, many priests are adamant that Maryam will not enter the temple with them, fiercely debating her presence. The first priest declares, "Impossible! No girl has ever been allowed to serve the temple. No woman has ever entered this holy site." Yet others are more sympathetic, noting it has been a custom for ages for children to be allowed to enter and serve the temple. But another priest intervenes, objecting that this time the child is a girl, and women are forbidden to enter. Zakariyya comes up with a solution that Maryam can worship and serve the temple but in a separate house away from the other worshippers. The idea gains traction, and Zakariyya is shown cutting a tree and building the house with his own hands with the help of a friend and supporter.

Zakariyya brings Maryam to the temple on a mule with the townspeople looking on. The townspeople slowly begin to gaze on her as she approaches, noting that she is Maryam, the daughter of ʿImran. As they reach the temple, Zakariyya takes her off the mule, and she begins to climb the steps. The camera focuses on her feet as she slowly moves up each step, a larger metaphor of women slowly rising to positions of power. The townspeople have become completely silent, and the high priests look on uneasily from above as a female approaches. As Maryam reaches the last step, she pauses and looks at all the priests, examining them and announcing her presence. She then takes the final step into the temple with dramatic music playing in the background and a loud bang. Maryam moves closer to the temple and bows in prostration with respect and admiration. The scene captures the radical moment of a woman entering the temple for the first time and challenging the patriarchal structure.

Maryam eventually grows up and becomes well known to the town and the surrounding area as a pious individual and miracle worker, and many come to visit the temple just for her to heal them. A woman, for instance, sees Maryam walking at night and grabs her cloak, pleading for her to help her sick son. None of the doctors has been able to help, and she asks Maryam for a piece of bread to cure him. Maryam listens to the crying mother, gives her a piece of bread, and states that she will pray for her son. However, it appears that Maryam is giving her own food to the townspeople while fasting and not feeding herself. She returns to her quarters and faints in exhaustion and hunger. When she awakes, fruits miraculously appear in her room, and she begins to eat them, a reference to the Qur'anic narrative (3:37).

Zakariyya comes into the room, sees the fruits, and asks Maryam where she got them, at first not receiving an answer. In the meantime, the priests and their associates continue to target Zakariyya, highlighting the fact that he doesn't have any children and that he will die completely alone and with no successor. They even send messengers to his house, making fun of his wife, Elizabeth, for not being able to conceive a child, which makes her dejected and depressed. Zakariyya begins to cry and prays, "I cannot bear these insults. Send me a sign to soothe my broken heart." He looks up, sees Maryam's house, and goes to visit her. He then asks again, "Maryam, tell me where these food and fruits have come from . . . who brings you these?" Maryam responds in the words of the Qur'an 3:37 that "these are from God; God bestows countless blessings to those he has chosen." Zakariyya realizes that his answer to having a child is to pray and speak to God: "You have taught this to me in my old age through Maryam." After his reflection, Zakariyya intently enters the temple, prays to have a child, and is granted a son, Yahya.

Maryam continues to perform miracles by God's will and challenges the priests' authority and dominion by praying in the temple and claiming that she communicates directly with God. Eventually, Zakariyya becomes an outcast, and Maryam encounters Gabriel/Jibril, who tells her that she will give birth to a pure boy. Maryam struggles to tell Zakariyya the news and finally decides not to as she retreats to the desert. She falls on a palm tree and states, "I wish I was dead. I wish people had forgotten me. I wish people never had heard of Maryam and never remember me again," which alludes to the chapter of Maryam (19:23). After the birth of her child, she feels the aftereffects, and a voice informs her of the stream beneath her and to shake the palm tree for dates. She is ordered to return to her people, but she worries that no one will believe her story and that the townspeople will shun her child. Nonetheless, she reconciles herself and states, "But if this is my Lord's command, I shall obey." She is then commanded to take a vow of silence and told that "your child will do the rest in the name of God."

The movie climaxes in the final scene, where Maryam returns to her people carrying baby 'Isa. Since she has made a vow of silence, she does not talk to anybody and refuses to respond to her people's questions and accusations. Some ask inquisitively and in disbelief, "Why have you done this? We placed all our hope in you" and "What am I seeing, Maryam? How can it be?" Others are more accusatory, screaming, "You have committed a grave sin; you are a sinner, a sinner!" The assault is led by one of the high priests, who doubted Maryam all along and now is using the opportunity to take her down and reassert his authority. He begins his monologue by stating, "She pretended to be innocent and helpful. But what do we see now?" One of his associates follows and paraphrases the Qur'anic verse (19:28), highlighting that "your father was not a bad man, and your mother was not a whore; what shame have you brought with you?"

An idea emerges that they must burn her alive to purify her, as that is the punishment for daughters of priests who have gone astray, a thought that gains currency from the crowd. The high priest continues to demand her to speak and defend herself, but Maryam is committed to the vow of silence. She points with her head to the child, to which the high priest laughs and asks, "Should we ask him?" He then continues to mock the proposal, asking the crowd, "She wants us to talk to this child" and then declaring, "Can you see where this has led?" He approaches the child, asking sarcastically, "Who are you, child? Introduce yourself." Dramatic music begins to play, and the narrator states that the child starts to speak, quoting the verses from the Qur'an (19:30–33) where Jesus announces that he is a servant of God and that God has given him a book and made him a prophet; he will cherish his pure mother and prosper. The high priests are in shock and disbelief and literally and metaphorically begin to fall down, screaming and crying. On the other hand, those who had hope and belief come closer to Maryam and 'Isa to rejoice and cry tears of joy. Their hope in the Messiah has finally come true, and the believers begin to kneel, recognizing Maryam's righteousness and the arrival of their savior. The movie concludes with Maryam smiling and holding her baby, 'Isa, with the sunrise in the background. The narrator quotes a Qur'anic verse: "Thus I chose Maryam and her son as a miracle, and as a sign for all of the people of the world."

The film not only is a historical drama but also questions the role of the clergy within contemporary society, especially in the Iranian Republic, which operates under the political system of the rule of the religious jurist (*wilayat al-faqih*). It could be seen as part of a series of other films that "critically examine the lofty positions [religious clergy members] enjoy in society, which in turn serves only to further emphasize their hierarchical relationship with the laity."[37] The film uses Maryam to articulate debates on the role of clergy within society, "including some of the more contentious issues that have otherwise been difficult to discuss publicly inside Iran."[38] The film compares the institutionalized morals and ideals of the priests with the realities of the everyday lives of the masses and how they are often at odds with empowering those who are poor and marginalized. While the priests in the film are technically "Jewish," they could easily be replaced by a Muslim clergy that seeks to repress dissent and prevent structural and revolutionary change throughout Muslim-majority countries. Although rooted in Qur'anic and historical reality, the film succeeds in presenting an "alternative way of understanding religion," where the spirituality of women and the masses is honored and recognized.[39]

It is important to note that the film does not critique religion as a whole or promote secularism as a means of liberation. Maryam's caretaker, Zakariyya, is one of the main characters and part of the religious establishment, a respected clergy member and prophet. Nonetheless, Zakariyya differs from the others in that he is more open to personal spirituality, miracles of the believer, and the potential of women. Rather, the director uses Maryam to challenge a particular type of religiosity that empowers male religious clerics who ally themselves with political power to the detriment of the masses. The director endorses a personal spirituality that challenges institutional authority, similar to what we saw earlier with Rabi'a al-'Adawiyya, who teaches older male religious scholars spiritual lessons about one's relationship to God. Instead of quoting from scripture or referencing scholarly works, Maryam demonstrates spirituality through sincerity, piety, and miracles.

---

37. Pak-Shiraz, *Shi'i Islam in Iranian Cinema*, 70.

38. Pak-Shiraz, *Shi'i Islam in Iranian Cinema*, 70.

39. Pak-Shiraz, *Shi'i Islam in Iranian Cinema*, 196.

## Documentary: *The Great Muslim American Road Trip*

Maryam also appears in documentary films, such as those about the Muslim American experience and interfaith encounters. In the documentary *The Great Muslim American Road Trip*, rap artist and host Mona Hayder and her husband, Sebastian Robins, take a road trip on Route 66, learning about Muslim American life, history, and culture.[40] Along the way, they make a stop in New Mexico at the Basilica of Saint Francis, one of the oldest churches in the United States. Built in 1626, it is home to a statue of the Virgin Mary from the 1400s. The camera follows Mona and Sebastian as they enter the church, gazing at the statue of Mary in reverence. Mona states, "Muslims don't make art of religious figures" but continues to explain that "what many people don't know is that Mary is very important in Islam." The camera then zooms in on the ancient statue of Mary.

The film quickly transitions to another scene where Sebastian is talking to one of the Basilica's teachers, who shares his experience at the house of the Virgin Mary in Turkey, the place where she is believed to have lived her last days. He narrates that when he visited the house during the Eid holiday, he saw hundreds of Muslims visiting the pilgrimage site. He began to wonder, "Why would all of these Muslims come on their holiday?"[41] He then read the Qur'an and realized that the scripture views Mary as one of the purest women. While he is speaking, the camera shows an English translation of the Qur'an and a hand opening to the chapter of Maryam and related verses on her. In particular, the camera focuses on verse 3:42: "Behold! the Angels said: 'O Mary! God hath chosen thee and purified thee—chosen thee above the women of all nations.'" The verse appears in translation in Old English style and in a font similar to that of the King James Bible.

The scene cuts to Mona having a discussion with the rector of the Basilica, Father Timothy Martinez. They sit facing each other within the nave, or sitting area, with the Basilica visible in the background.

---

40. Alex Kronemer, dir., *The Great Muslim American Road Trip* (PBS, 2022).

41. The house of the Virgin Mary will be discussed in more detail in the next chapter.

Mona shares that people frequently ask her as a Muslim what her relationship with Jesus and Mary is, and she explains that she has a "deep and devoted connection to them in their relationship . . . Mary as mother and Jesus as her son." Mona discusses Maryam in the Qur'an and states how she is "devoted, righteous and blessed." As Mona speaks, the scene fades back to the Qur'an, where verse 3:43 appears: "O Mary, worship thy Lord devoutly: Prostrate thyself, and bow down (in prayer) with those who bow down." Mona continues to explain that Maryam is an "inspiration to her in the way that she was tender and loving and devoted to God so much so that she could raise a child that could change the entire world." As Mona speaks, the camera captures the reaction of Father Timothy, who is nodding and visibly moved.

Father Martinez then shares his favorite story about Mary: When Jesus and his apostles go to a wedding, Mary comes and says, "They have run out of wine."[42] For a long time, Father Martinez didn't understand the story but later learned that hospitality was an essential part of the culture during Jesus's time. If somebody got a reputation of being inhospitable, they would "kick you out of town." Mary was, therefore, speaking out of concern for the young couple who was running the risk of starting their marriage in a tragedy. As Father Martinez speaks, the camera shows Mary's painting within the Basilica, demonstrating that her legacy is still present. He connects the story to Mona's reflection, agreeing that Mary was that "tender woman . . . God, oh God, yes." Father Martinez concludes by asking, "What love drives people to do that?" and show compassion and care for others. He ends by stating that he "wants to be that type of person." Throughout the reflection, the camera captures the reactions by Mona, who is similarly listening intently and nodding in understanding.

After the discussion, Mona is back on the road with her husband, reflecting on her conversation. She notes that Father Martinez had a "beautiful sense of humor and giggled when he talked" but at the same time was "very reverential and devoted . . . very beautiful." After Sebastian emphasizes the importance of Jesus in Islam, Mona starts to

42. John 2:1–11.

talk about Maryam's birth story, which is "so powerful; it is this thing that connects women across all cultures. It doesn't matter who you are or where you are; if you have experienced birth, you have a story to tell that can immediately connect to somebody else." As Mona speaks, images of diverse women appear on the screen, with Mona rapping about motherhood and standing reverentially in front of the statue of Mary. The scene connects Maryam to various women around the world and Mona's art and spirituality.

Mona continues that "that chapter of the Qur'an is so moving, that her labor and her labor pains, and pain and her crying out to God is sacred and so sacred that it made it into the scripture." As Mona speaks, the Qur'an once again appears in English translation, specifically verses 19:23–24: "And the pains of childbirth drove her to the trunk of a palm-tree. She cried (in her anguish): 'Ah! Would that I had died before this! Would that I had been a thing forgotten and out of sight! But (a voice) cried to her from beneath the (palm-tree): 'Grieve not! For thy Lord hath provided a rivulet beneath thee." The scene intentionally displays not only verse 19:23, which details her labor pains, but also verse 19:24, which describes God's response to her calls of pain and anguish. Specifically, "Grieve not," from 19:24, is emphasized, with the statement calming Maryam's fears and distress.

The documentary thus generally affirms Islamic aniconism by depicting the Christian statue of the Virgin Mary but not any Muslim ones. When Maryam is discussed, the Qur'an is opened, and relevant verses about her distinctiveness and devotion are displayed. However, when Father Martinez speaks, a Christian painting of Mary from the Basilica is shown. Nonetheless, there are times when Mona speaks about Maryam and is shown standing in front of the Christian statue of Mary, demonstrating the connection between the two religions. She is not iconoclastic or disturbed by the image but sees its value and meaning for both Christians and Muslims. Moreover, while Mona and Father Martinez cite different sources, they both share how Mary inspires them in their modern lives. For

Mona, in particular, Maryam is a model for her as a modern spiritual woman and mother. Instead of depicting Maryam, Mona and diverse Muslim women appear, demonstrating that Maryam's legacy and memory continue to live on. Specifically, Mona becomes a "modern Maryam" who embodies the Qur'anic teachings and her ecumenical and bridge-building potential.

## Conclusion

The depictions of Maryam in Islamic art and film range from those that endorse aniconism to those that fully depict her. Maryam was not considered a prophet by most scholars, thus allowing her to be represented in ways that prophets were traditionally not. Nonetheless, the various depictions support the idea of Maryam as her own figure and protagonist, similar to how the Qur'an and prophet traditions represent her. Maryam is the primary focus of the various artists, whether as a nourisher, an ancestral mother, or a spiritual guide. The various depictions of Maryam build on those found in the textual sources and provide visual examples of how she inspired people in classical times and continues to do so today.

CHAPTER SIX

# Maryam in Contemporary Times

MARYAM DOES NOT simply exist within history but also in contemporary times. Many of the themes discussed in the previous chapters have continued into the twentieth and twenty-first centuries, such as the focus on spirituality, scripture, and miracles. However, there is a modern shift in Maryam's appearance in discussions of women and women's rights, ecumenism and interfaith, and global peace and prosperity. These modern movements build on the classical sources and expand the textual and scholastic traditions in new and innovative ways.

## Meryem Ana Evi and Vatican II's *Nostra Aetate*

While Maryam has historically been shared between Christians and Muslims, there is a greater effort in contemporary times to emphasize pilgrimage sites that unite the two religions. Meryem Ana Evi is such a site near Ephesus, Turkey, where it is believed that Maryam could have lived her last years in the ancient city and within the home. For instance, St. John, who was entrusted to take care of Maryam, later died in the city, and his tomb is found there.[1] Moreover, the first Basilica dedicated to Mary is in Ephesus, and in 431, an ecumenical council defined the dogma on the divine motherhood of Mary within the space.[2] The

1. John 19:27.

2. Zafer Öter and Mehmet Yavuz Çetinkaya, "Interfaith Tourist Behaviour at Religious Heritage Sites: House of the Virgin Margin Mary Case in Turkey," *International Journal of Religious Tourism and Pilgrimage* 4, no. 4 (2016), 4. Simge Komurcu and Özgür Saribas, "The Feeling of the Visitors Participating in Religious Tourism: The Case of Virgin Mary In Izmir," *International Journal of Contemporary*

pilgrimage site was created in the late nineteenth century based on the visions of a peasant woman, which eventually led a group of priests to discover a house.[3] The pilgrimage site eventually attracted attention after World War II, in an era of religious revival and global peace. While initially viewed as a "Christian" site, many Muslims began to visit, and it now has over one million visitors annually from both religious groups.[4]

The brick structure has prominent arches demonstrating its age and ancient quality. A tree shoots out of the side of the building near the entrance, greeting the visitors. Within the house, there are two rooms representing both Christian and Muslim values and arts. On the Christian side, a statue of Mary is found along with icons, candles, and sanctuary lamps. A black statue of Mary appears within a niche with arches surrounding her and embracing her presence. However, on the Muslim side, there are no statues, thus representing Islamic aniconism. Rather, we find the Qur'anic chapter of Maryam inscribed, manifesting the Islamic emphasis on the word and oral expression. Many Christians and Muslims come to the shrine with various petitions ranging from financial challenges to childbearing. They "light candles in the shrine, drink holy water from the spring, and attach strips of cloth with prayers to a nearby prayer wall."[5]

Christian theologians have referenced it as a site of "shared devotion," and it even appears to be alluded to in the Vatican II document Nostra Aetate (1965), where several sections speak about Muslims: "They [Muslims] honor Mary, his virgin mother; at times they even

---

*Economics and Administrative Sciences* 6, no. 1–2 (2016): 31–42. Komurcu and Saribas note that the dominant feeling at the site, according to respondents, is that "they feel peaceful, spiritual, faithful, loyal, devote, solemness, blessed, honored, engulfed, inspired after their journey."

3. Donal Carroll, *Mary's House: The Extraordinary Story Behind the Discovery of the House Where the Virgin Mary Lived and Died* (Christian Classics, 2002).

4. Rita George-Tvrtkovič, *Christians, Muslims, and Mary: A History* (Paulist Press 2018), 122.

5. George-Tvrtkovič, *Christians, Muslims, and Mary*, 123.

call on her with devotion."[6] The statement reflects the observation of Christians, specifically Catholics, on how Muslims refer to Maryam and relate to her, such as visiting the various shrines devoted to her.

This observation likely represents a personal connection that many Christians had with Muslims by speaking directly to them or seeing their religious practice rather than a statement based simply on Islamic texts. Specifically, this statement in Nostra Aetate was influenced by what bishops had seen at Meryem Ana Evi, where Christians and Muslims both visited the site with reverence and devotion. As the mid-twentieth-century French missionary Yves Plumey observed, "[Muslims] piously visit Marian sanctuaries, take part in processions honoring her, devoutly honor her images, often name their daughters after her and implore her protection everywhere: these things are very frequently reported in India, Pakistan, Mozambique, Egypt, Iran, Turkey, and most especially in Ephesus, where the government kindly approves and allows the opportunity."[7]

Even though Plumey was stationed in Cameroon, Africa, he was in touch with Christians from the Middle East and South Asia who witnessed devotion to Maryam in various ways, from names to depictions. He speaks about the entire Muslim world but makes a special reference to the Virgin Mary House near Ephesus, which is sanctioned and protected by the Turkish government.[8]

6. George-Tvrtkovič, *Christians, Muslims, and Mary*, 122.

7. George-Tvrtkovič, *Christians, Muslims, and Mary*, 138. See also Rita George-Tvrtkovič, "Bridge or Barrier? Mary and Islam in William of Tripoli and Nicholas of Cusa," *Medieval Encounters* 22 (2016): 307–325. See George-Tvrtkovič's works in general for more discussions on how Mary was both a bridge and barrier in the premodern and modern worlds.

8. The last section, "they even call on her with devotion," appears intentionally ambiguous, as many Muslims condemn intercession and reject making supplications directly to her. Such practices could be considered polytheistic (*shirk*) and be perceived to violate Islam's central theological tenet of absolute monotheism (*tawhid*). However, as discussed, Maryam is a universally revered figure within Islam, and Muslims around the world are devoted to her. Her figure is a source of inspiration for those facing difficult times such as childbirth and desperation.

The statement on Maryam fits within the larger section of Nostra Aetate regarding Muslims: "The church has also a high regard for the Muslims. They worship God, who is one, living and subsistent, merciful and almighty, the Creator of heaven and earth, who has also spoken to humanity. They endeavor to submit themselves without reserve to the hidden decrees of God, just as Abraham submitted himself to God's plan, to whose faith Muslims eagerly link their own."[9] Maryam is thus referenced alongside Abraham, who is also seen as a model of faith, submission, and spirituality.[10]

The Catholic Church affirms that Muslims worship one God who is "merciful and almighty" and "spoke to humanity." Such descriptions are apt regarding the chapter and story of Maryam, where the name of God "the Merciful" is frequently used and Jibril spoke directly to Maryam.[11] Through this description, the Catholic Church depicted Muslims through a theological lens, not simply one of politics, violence, and conquest reminiscent of Islamophobic tropes that are pervasive today.

---

9. For more on Nostra Aetate, see Kail Ellis, ed., *Nostra Aetate, Non-Christian Religions, and Interfaith Relations* (Palgrave Macmillan, 2021).

10. For a discussion of Abraham as a common figure within discussions of Catholicism and Islam, see Wilhelmus G. B. M. Valkenberg, "A Faithful Christian Interpretation of Islam," in *Faithful Interpretations: Truth and Islam in Catholic Theology of Religions*, ed. Philip Geister and Gösta Hallonsten (The Catholic University of America Press, 2021). Valkenberg argues that Christians should see Muslims as theological partners even if they disagree on the nature of God and scripture. Christian Krokus, *The Theology of Louis Massignon: Islam, Christ, and the Church* (The Catholic University of America Press, 2017). Krokus also discusses how a mid-twentieth-century Catholic scholar of Islam, Louis Massignon, believed that Islam was a "Abrahamic schism" and how the term *Abrahamic religions* can be attributed to the scholar.

11. Nonetheless, as Daniel Madigan points out, the council chose to speak about Muslims rather than Islam per se and thus evade questions relating to Islamic theology and practices. As he explains, "The Council thus avoids discussion of the issues of Muhammad, the Qur'àn, the Shari'a, etc., in favour of a recognition of the positive elements in the life of the Muslim believer." Daniel A. Madigan, "Nostra Aetate and the Questions It Chose to Leave Open," *Gregorianum* 87, no. 4 (2006): 781–796.

Christians and Muslims have both used the site as a platform to speak about interreligious affairs and ecumenical relations. For instance, the Turkish government actively maintains the house as a way of asserting its commitment to religious diversity, preserving history, and fostering interfaith dialogue. In 2006, Pope Benedict XVI spoke at the site about the unrest in the holy land and called for peace: "Strengthened by God's word, from here in Ephesus, a city blessed by the presence of Mary Most Holy—who we know is loved and venerated also by Muslims—let us lift up to the Lord a special prayer for peace between peoples."[12] Here, the pope emphasized Mary as somebody "who we know is loved and venerated also by Muslims" and could bridge different people and bring peace to the volatile region. He continued, "From this edge of the Anatolian peninsula, a natural bridge between continents, let us implore peace and reconciliation, above all for those dwelling in the Land called 'Holy' and considered as much by Christians, Jews and Muslims alike: it is the land of Abraham, Isaac and Jacob, destined to be the home of a people that would become a blessing for all the nations (cf. Gen 12:1–3). Peace for all of humanity!"[13]

With these words, Pope Benedict attempted to use the site of Ephesus to address the issue of the "holy land," or that of Israel and Palestine, and the challenges of violence that the world was witnessing at the time. To speak for peace, he emphasizes common figures, not just Mary but also "Abraham, Isaac and Jacob," who are shared by "Christians, Jews and Muslims alike." He also highlights the place of Meryem Ana Evi in Anatolia, which is a "natural bridge" between continents and people. The house of the Meryem Ana Evi is important not only because it celebrates Mary—a common link between Christians and Muslims—but also because it is located in Turkey, a bridge between civilizations. The figure of Mary and the place of Anatolia thus help bring people together in unique and historical ways.

---

12. Joseph Ellul, "The Issue of Muslim-Christian Dialogue 'Nostra Aetate' Revisited," *Angelicum* 84, no. 2 (2007): 378.

13. Ellul, "The Issue of Muslim-Christian Dialogue," 378.

The messages of Nostra Aetate and the Meryem Ana Evi are even reflected in the statements of Pope Francis. Pope Francis's use of Mary comes in the context of a more general speech, in which he addresses the issue of Muslim immigrants, Christian minorities, and dialogue. In his various statements, he makes positive comments about Islam and Muslims in light of Jesus and Mary: "The sacred writings of Islam have retained some Christian teachings; Jesus and Mary receive profound veneration and it is admirable to see how Muslims both young and old, men and women, make time for daily prayer and faithfully take part in religious services."[14] It is significant here that the pope groups Jesus and Mary together, which is similar to how the Qur'an pairs them, such as in the common Qur'anic phrase "'Isa ibn Maryam" ("Jesus the son of Mary").[15] The pope emphasizes that Muslims "retain some Christian teachings" and discusses their "profound veneration" of Jesus and Mary, a possible reference to Meryem Ana Evi and other forms of Muslim devotion. He states that it is "admirable" to see both young and old Muslims, men and women, dedicate time to daily prayer and participate in religious services. Islam is not a religion of the elderly or males but includes many youths and women. The pope commends Muslims for making prayer and religious services a priority and part of their daily schedule, especially in increasingly secular societies. In doing so, the pope goes beyond the words of Nostra Aetate by emphasizing commonalities and differences and stressing moral action and a community of believers.[16]

---

14. The Royal Aal Al-Bayt Institute for Islamic Thought, *A Common Word: Between Us and You* (Al Manhal, 2013); Moussa Serge Hyacinthe Traore, "Pope Francis Describes What Is True and Holy in Islam," *Journal of Ecumenical Studies* 56, no. 2 (2021): 252.

15. Traore, "Pope Francis Describes," 263.

16. Jerusha Tanner Rhodes, "Beyond the Rays of Truth? Nostra Aetate, Islam, and the Value of Difference," in *The Future of Interreligious Dialogue: A Multireligious Conversation on Nostra Aetate*, ed. C. L. Cohen, P. F. Knitter, and U. Rosenhagen (Orbis, 2017).

## A Common Word

Maryam also appears within documents on Christian-Muslim relations that have been initiated by Muslims, such as "A Common Word" (ACW), completed in 2007, only a few years after 9/11 and amid the Iraq War.[17] ACW has been called the "Islamic Nostra Aetate" in that it represents a Muslim self-understanding of Christianity and seeks common ground between the two great religions.[18] It articulates this climate in its introduction and conclusion, stating, "Muslims and Christians together make up well over half of the world's population. Without peace and justice between these two religious communities, there can be no meaningful peace in the world. The future of the world depends on peace between Muslims and Christians." It further emphasizes that there is "terrible weaponry of the modern world" and that "no side can unilaterally win a conflict between more than half of the world's inhabitants. Thus, our common future is at stake. The very survival of the world itself is perhaps at stake." The ACW initiative was "rooted in global Islam," and thus the "impact of ACW has also been global."[19] The aim was not polemical or apologetic but instead sought to identify what it "finds to be common ground, namely, the

17. For more on the context of ACW and Christian responses, see Yvonne Yazbeck Haddad and Jane I. Smith, "The Quest for 'A Common Word': Initial Christian Responses to a Muslim Initiative," *Islam and Christian–Muslim Relations* 20, no. 4 (2009): 369–388.

18. Vebjørn L. Horsfjord, "A Common Word," in *Routledge Handbook on Christian-Muslim Relations*, ed. David Thomas (Routledge, 2018), 258–265. As Horsfjord states of "A Common Word," "The text outlines an Islamic understanding of the relationship between the two faiths and provides a basis on which Muslims can approach their Christian counterparts with both respect for the other and confidence in their own tradition. Christians would not be required to agree or even to discuss the theology of the document in much detail. In this case *A Common Word* could be seen as reciprocating *Nostra Aetate*, the declaration from the Second Vatican Council which outlines a Christian (Catholic) understanding of other religions, including Islam," 262. See article for a background and responses to ACW.

19. Lejla Demiri, *The Future of Interfaith Dialogue: Muslim-Christian Encounters Through A Common Word*, ed. Yazid Said and Lejla Demiri (Cambridge University Press, 2018), 2.

two shared principles of love of God and love of neighbour, on the basis of which may venture a theological engagement shared by mutual trust and friendship."[20] Similar to Nostra Aetate, ACW sought relational engagement with the religious other that was not simply based on texts and scripture.

The document mentions Maryam and her Qur'anic chapter several times to articulate Islamic values and to connect with Christians. In its introductory section, it speaks about the chapter of the Opening (*surat al-Fatiha*), which is recited by Muslims in their daily prayers and concludes with a prayer of "grace and guidance." The authors argue that this prayer is connected to "salvation and love," which is related to a verse in the chapter of Maryam: "Lo! those who believe and do good works, the Infinitely Good will appoint for them love." As discussed in chapter 1, the chapter of Maryam is the only one that contains the particular word for *love* (*widd*) and the most extended narrative of Maryam's life and story. Maryam once again appears in the discussion of how Christians should not see Muslims as against but instead with them. Muslims recognize Jesus Christ as the Messiah but in the following way: "The Messiah Jesus son of Mary is a Messenger of God and His Word which he cast unto Mary and a Spirit from Him" (Al-Nisa', 4:171). The verse, like other Qur'anic ones, emphasizes that 'Isa is the "son of Mary" and a product of "His word which he cast unto Mary." Maryam thus appears as a way to affirm 'Isa's messengerhood and miracle.

Several years after the completion of the ACW, the lead writer of the document, Prince Ghazi bin Muhammad of Jordan, offered a reflection about a "solitary tree" in the eastern Jordanian desert and its connection to Christian-Muslim relations.[21] The tree is 1,500 years old and a type of pistachio tree found in Jordan and its surrounding areas. He explains that the ACW was born under that tree in that he and a group of scholars went to the tree and prayed underneath it to make

20. Demiri, *The Future of Interfaith Dialogue*, 3.

21. Miroslav Volf, Ghazi bin Muhammad, and Melissa Yarrington, *A Common Word: Muslims and Christians on Loving God and Neighbor* (W. B. Eerdmans, 2010), 3.

ACW a success. At the end of the chapter, Prince Ghazi connects the tree to the Qur'an and the story of Maryam. The Qur'an states that a "good word is like a good tree, its roots set firm and its branches in the heaven, giving its fruits in every season by the permission of the Lord."[22] Just like a tree, words can grow, branch out, and bear fruit that nourishes and enriches the world. He further stated that it is no coincidence that Maryam, "for both Muslims and Christians, the greatest woman who ever lived . . . is described as having birth pangs under a tree." He further cited verses in the chapter of Maryam about her labor and birth and how she shook the tree to receive relief and aid. Thus, Prince Ghazi sees himself in the light of Maryam, where she seeks divine support and assistance under a tree and connects both Christians and Muslims.

When Nostra Aetate and ACW are compared, it can be seen that both documents appeared after major conflicts: Nostra Aetate after World War II and the creation of Israel, and ACW after 9/11 and the Iraq War. While both focus on theological similarities and differences, they respond to specific cultural and political developments related to land and resources. Moreover, the documents appear to have been written independently and do not necessarily respond to each other. Nostra Aetate was influenced by bishops who lived among Muslims, while ACW was influenced by Muslims who had studied Christian and Islamic traditions alongside Christians. While both touch on Mary, there is still further potential to use her as a common link and bridge between the two world religions.

## Christian Exegesis and Theological Responses

Maryam appears not only in official statements but also in Christian exegeses of the Qur'an and theological responses. While Christians have engaged the Qur'an throughout its history, these readings were often in the context of polemics and interreligious debates. In contemporary times, Christian polemics continue, but we also see a new attempt to

22. Volf et al., *A Common Word*, 16.

provide Christian readings of Muslim scriptures that open new interpretations and theological possibilities.

For instance, Neal Robinson discusses how Muhammad's life and biography connect with the stories and memories of Jesus and Mary.[23] Robinson highlights how the Qur'an presents Maryam as an exemplar for the wives of the Prophet Muhammad and the believers in general. Specifically, she is mentioned in chapter 66, which alludes to a domestic dispute between Muhammad and his wives. The chapter also discusses righteous women of previous nations, whom the wives and the believing community could model themselves after: Maryam and Asiya, the wife of Pharaoh. The chapter ends by extolling Maryam: "Maryam, daughter of 'Imran. She guarded her chastity, so We breathed into her from Our spirit. She accepted the truth of her Lord's words and Scriptures: she was truly devout." Maryam's example of being "devout" represents an example for Muhammad's wives as well as all believers.

Robinson also observes that similar language is used to describe Maryam and the Prophet's wives, like 'Ayisha. For instance, according to Islamic tradition, the twenty-fourth Qur'anic chapter, "Light" (*Nur*), speaks about an accusation of 'Ayisha's infidelity. The Muslims were returning from a campaign where her howdah was loaded on a camel while she was not inside. She thus was left behind and brought back the next day by a "handsome young man" who had followed the caravan, which led to speculation and rumors that the two had slept together. The Qur'an refutes this accusation, stating that it was a "tremendous calumny" and that the rumor should not have been spread among the people. Similarly, Maryam is accused in the Qur'an of infidelity for having a child ('Isa) out of wedlock, leading to accusations from her people, who emphasize that she came from a good family and that her father was not a bad man and her mother was not unchaste. As it does with 'Ayisha, the Qur'an uses the phrase "tremendous calumny" to describe the charges against Maryam and defends her chastity and piety.

---

23. Neal Robinson, "Jesus and Mary in the Qur'ān: Some Neglected Affinities," *Religion* 20 (1990): 161–175.

Robinson further draws a connection between Maryam and Muhammad, noting the similarities in their stories and Qur'anic representation. An angel appears to them, often as a human being, to inform them of the wishes of God. For Maryam, it was the birth of 'Isa, while for Muhammad, it was the Qur'anic revelations. They receive revelation and divine commands from behind a curtain (*hijab*) and in seclusion. In the chapter of Maryam, she is behind a curtain and alone when the messenger appears, informing her of the forthcoming birth of 'Isa. The Qur'an explains that Muhammad only receives revelation through inspiration, messenger, or behind a curtain. Maryam and Muhammad thus receive divine commandments and revelation in similar ways and have parallel archetypes and revelatory stories.[24]

Likewise, Rev. Daniel Madigan, SJ does not see Muhammad in competition with Jesus but rather as a type of Mary. He contends that many Christians are hesitant to speak about or affirm Muhammad as a prophet because it would, in some ways, diminish the role of Jesus and his salvific nature. However, Madigan contends that the "Muslim faith does not claim that Muhammad is the Word, but rather that he is the human channel through whom the Word entered the world."[25] He continues to explain, "In this respect, he is a parallel to Mary in the Christian scheme of things—the human person whose cooperation was needed to give flesh to the Word."[26] Just like Muhammad brought the Qur'an, Maryam brought Jesus, and he represents the "words of God" in their respective religions. Madigan cites Seyyed Hossein Nasr, who has pointed out that Mary's virginity affirms that Jesus's birth was a divine miracle, just as Muhammad's illiteracy signals that the Qur'an is a divine revelation as well.[27]

---

24. Maryam and Muhammad also seek refuge from Satan so as not to deviate or be led astray.

25. Madigan, "Nostra Aetate and the Questions It Chose to Leave Open," 793.

26. Madigan, "Nostra Aetate and the Questions It Chose to Leave Open," 793.

27. Madigan, "Nostra Aetate and the Questions It Chose to Leave Open," 793.

In another piece, "Mary and Muhammad: Bearers of the Word," Madigan continues the argument that Mary and Muhammad are both "channels for the divine Word rather than creators or authors of it" since Muhammad is considered "illiterate" and Mary a "virgin."[28] However, to make the "word" divine, God needed a human vehicle, the "voice" of Muhammad and the womb of Mary. Yet the human element doesn't overtake the divine one. While they are included in revelation, "both characters are completely involved in the process of revelation and yet also in a way strangely excluded from it."[29] There is no doubt that Jesus comes from Mary and the Qur'an emerges from Muhammad's mouth, but the two figures' roles are sometimes not explored or critically examined.

Madigan expands on the comparison of Mary and Muhammad, noting a number of similarities.[30] Mary is an orphan-like figure in the Qur'an, needing a guardian, and her father is never mentioned. She receives divine revelation and communication unsolicited, and the experience is fearful and unexpected. The angel Jibril is seen as the intermediary who bears God's commands and words. The "word" speaks up and defends his mother from accusations of adultery and unchastity and defines itself and mission. In a similar way, Muhammad was an orphan whose uncle Abu Talib became his guardian, took care of him, and raised him to maturity. He unexpectedly receives divine revelation from the angel Jibril in the cave Hira and is initially afraid and startled. The Qur'an speaks up to defend itself (its miraculous nature) and defines its mission and vision for humanity. Thus, Mary and Muhammad share a similar upbringing, contact with the divine, and message to humanity.

28. Daniel Madigan, "Mary and Muhammad: Bearers of the Word," *Australasian Catholic Record* 80, no. 4 (2003): 421.

29. Madigan, "Mary and Muhammad: Bearers of the Word," 421.

30. Madigan, "Mary and Muhammad: Bearers of the Word," 422.

## Comparative Theology

While Christians have responded theologically to Maryam, recent attempts have also been made to develop joint Christian and Muslim theological responses. In their book *Mary in the Qur'an*, Muna Tatari and Klaus von Stosch break new theological ground with what is, in "likelihood, the first work about Mary jointly written by a Muslim theologian and a Christian theologian."[31] The authors stress that the work was written "jointly" and is not a combination of two separate theologians and their personal views. The only separate entries are in the book's conclusion, where the authors summarize their findings based on their own theological commitments and worldviews. In their study, they both take advantage of literary studies of the Qur'an and Muslim exegeses but also use historical-critical methods that attempt to put the Qur'an in conversation with other texts and Christian movements of late antiquity.

In his conclusion, von Stosch shares his reflections on Mary in the Qur'an and how it complicated and enriched his own Christian faith and understanding of her. He was impressed by the "great esteem in which Mary is held in the Qur'an, which is reaffirmed time and again in moving and poetic words throughout Islamic history, intensifies my own high regard and love for Mary."[32] In the Christian tradition, she lives in dialogue and familiarity with God, and he found it "wonderful" that these are reinforced and attested in the Qur'an as well. She is an "extreme example of human independence" in that she relies solely on God and is a loving mother in both the Qur'an and the Bible.[33]

Specifically, von Stosch outlines the discussion of Maryam as a prophet in the Islamic tradition[34] as enriching, as he never conceived

31. Muna Tatari and Klaus von Stosch, *Mary in the Qur'an: Friend of God, Virgin, Mother*, trans. Peter Lewis (Gingko, 2021). See also the earlier Nilo Geagea, *Mary of the Koran: A Meeting Point between Christianity and Islam*, trans. Lawrence Fares (Philosophical Library, 1984).

32. Tatari and von Stosch, *Mary in the Qur'an*, 285.

33. Tatari and von Stosch, *Mary in the Qur'an*, 285.

34. See chapter 4.

of a prophet "with attributes such as approachability, weakness, vulnerability, and tolerance of ambiguity."[35] The discussion of Maryam's potential prophecy led von Stosch to reexamine prophecy within the Christian context and the Bible, where prophets are often seen as a prefiguration of Christ rather than through their own autonomy and struggles. As he states, "The figures of the male and female prophets of the Bible have the capacity to show us a way to a deeper and better understanding of Christ rather than simply reflect what we already know about Christ." He further was reawakened to Marian piety and devotion, which made him "reappraise Marian piety within my own Catholic tradition with a fresh eye." Through the Qur'an, he "rediscovered" Mary as "indissolubly linked with Jesus Christ": Jesus as a source of salvation and Mary as a sign of God's presence for all nations and peoples.

Moreover, von Stosch realized how the Qur'an decouples Mary from imperialist theologies and as one who wins "wars on behalf of the powerful." Instead, she steps in to assist those who have been marginalized and plays an "emancipatory" role in the Qur'an. Part of her role is to be "transgressive" and not fit neatly within particular categories and roles: "Time and again, Mary breaks down simple dichotomies."[36] While Mary is often subsumed under the "traditional" camp, she could be a "pacesetter of modernity" in that she is providing new ways for men to think about gender and relationships and male power.[37]

Mary is also seen as a "bridging figure" who can link the three great Abrahamic religions. She is part of a practicing Jewish family, gives birth to Jesus, and is subsumed under the banner of Islam. In contrast, the Christian Mary often becomes a point of contention between Jews and Christians regarding her chastity and birthing a new religion. For von Stosch, this bridging does not only have to be among religions

35. Tatari and von Stosch, *Mary in the Qur'an*, 286.

36. Tatari and von Stosch, *Mary in the Qur'an*, 288.

37. Von Stosch notes that Mary could be seen as not only the "Queen of Heaven" but also the "Queer of Heaven."

only but can even be a bridge in the "ongoing conversations between Christian denominations."[38] The Islamic Mary may give Protestants a new window to appreciate her role with Christ and within Christianity, while liberal and conservative Catholics may be able to see both radical and traditional aspects within her. This ecumenism may be bolstered by the fact that Maryam has an "impressive independence," as she needs no male provider and has an outward, expressive nature regarding her faith. In an age when religion is often considered private, she demonstrates that religion can be expressive and public.

Maryam further disrupts certain Christian doctrines regarding the relationship between virginity and divinity. Von Stosch explains that he was taught that the virginity of Mary was intimately connected with Jesus's divinity. However, we see that the Qur'an "affirms the virginity of Mary while at the same time denying the divine nature of Jesus."[39] The Qur'an, therefore, affirms the miracle of Maryam's virginity while at the same time asserting the humanity and prophecy of ʿIsa. Maryam's miracle is one of the reasons she is chosen "above all other women," but she is at the same time "accessible, approachable and vulnerable."[40] Maryam thus becomes relatable rather than distant, remote, and a model of perfection.

Nonetheless, von Stosch finds certain aspects of his Christian faith relevant and essential to his own understanding of Mary. For instance, he explains that he appreciates the "conflict-laden" Mary presented in the Bible and with other biblical prophets. In the Bible, Mary had challenges dealing with her son's public ministry and only began to believe in Jesus as Christ "through a great deal of conflict and falling out."[41] He encourages Muslims to learn more about Mary's inner conflicts regarding her son and his future mission. Moreover, von Stosch shares that in his own life, he was able to "attest that the caring love of

38. Tatari and von Stosch, *Mary in the Qur'an*, 290.

39. Tatari and von Stosch, *Mary in the Qur'an*, 292.

40. Tatari and von Stosch, *Mary in the Qur'an*, 293.

41. Tatari and von Stosch, *Mary in the Qur'an*, 295.

God first became apparent to me in my mother."[42] In a similar way, "we bring God into the world, because Mary brought God into the world."[43] We see God's presence in the world and with those around us through worship and our relationship with others. Last, he sees the value of love connected to divine power, which becomes an "all-embracing reality." This love is not only connected with the divine but also "experienced in the love that we humans show for one another." In conclusion, he finds that the engagement with the Islamic Mary is a means to enable the Marian devotion of the church to "find its voice again."[44]

In her conclusion, Tatari outlines some of the key points that she benefits from the theological engagement and her Muslim background. She observes that Maryam "turns societal norms upside-down" and also has a political message that disrupts the established social order.[45] She further sees the connection between Muhammad and Mary in that Mary received 'Isa (the "word of God"), became pregnant with him, and brought him to the world as a message to her people. Similarly, Muhammad received the Qur'an (the "word of God"), recited it, and brought it to his people. Despite these parallels, Tatari is clear that Maryam is not given the title of "messenger" in the Qur'an, perhaps because it intended to emphasize her being a "sign of God" in the story and narrative. Nonetheless, the story of Maryam is "a comforting and inspiring example" and a "role model" for Muhammad, especially in the early Meccan era, when Muhammad was under attack verbally and physically and even had some of his followers travel to the Christian Abyssinia. Moreover, Muhammad was "shaken to the core" the first time he encountered the words of God and rushed home to his wife, Khadija, for "protection and solace." Similarly, Maryam was alone when

42. Tatari and von Stosch, *Mary in the Qur'an*, 295.

43. Tatari and von Stosch, *Mary in the Qur'an*, 295.

44. Tatari and von Stosch, *Mary in the Qur'an*, 296.

45. Tatari and von Stosch, *Mary in the Qur'an*, 299.

the angel Gabriel visited her, making her reliant on God in a "radical manner."[46]

The comparative theological approach made Tatari more focused on the idea of "grace" and how God gives and loves because of his essence and not because of human action and response. While Tatari benefited from medieval exegeses, she became critical of approaches that sought to interpret the Qur'an through triumphalism and polemics rather than within the history in which it was revealed. For instance, she discovered that during the time of the Qur'an, Mary was considered a quasi-divine figure within the imperial exploitation of the reign of Heraclius. The Qur'an was thus not simply theological in its stances regarding Mary but also a critique of how she was being used within political power and interests. Maryam further gave Tatari "the insight that there are as many different concepts of living as there are people in this world."[47] Like Rabi'a had previously explored, Maryam does not fit the ideal of a married woman with children but rather one who voluntarily becomes celibate for the love of God. In a similar way, Maryam gave Tatari the impetus to explore other figures, such as Eve or Hawa in the Islamic traditions. Hawa is held in esteem in the Qur'an and within Islamic tradition; the city of Jeddah in Saudi Arabia is even named after her. Tatari champions this respect and honor for the women "against the typecast manner in which they are disparaged in the Christian tradition."[48]

Similar to "A Common Word," Tatari emphasizes love as a bridge between various religions and theological worldviews. She ends the book by stating, "I too cannot help but see this key category of love as a radical category, a radical force guiding thinking, feelings and action."[49] Mary is a bridge figure, which enables Tatari to "appreciate the concept of loving devotion to God in all its radicalism" but also be grounded in understanding Islam as a "middle way" and the golden mean. For Tatari,

---

46. Tatari and von Stosch, *Mary in the Qur'an*, 301.

47. Tatari and von Stosch, *Mary in the Qur'an*, 309.

48. Tatari and von Stosch, *Mary in the Qur'an*, 310.

49. Tatari and von Stosch, *Mary in the Qur'an*, 311.

love appears throughout the story of Maryam, and her engagement with Christian scriptures and theologians only increases her love for her. She concludes, "It would be wonderful if our book gave Muslims and Christians the impetus to discover Mary afresh in her loving aspect: as a figure who is the focus of divine love and who shows us that love is the way forward."[50]

## Feminist Engagements

Along with theological engagements, Maryam appears in feminist readings, where she is used to advance women's rights and position within Muslim societies. For instance, Hosn Abboud surveys the scholars al-Qurtubi and Ibn Hazm, examined earlier,[51] to stress that they both believed Maryam was a prophet and equal or superior to men.[52] Abboud further tackles arguments against the idea of Maryam being a prophet, such as verse 12:109: "Nor did we send before thee (as apostles) any but men, Whom did we inspire (Men) living in habitations." As discussed in chapter 3, classical and modern Qur'anic commentators often use this verse to argue that prophecy is exclusive to men, as the word *men* (*rijal*) is used in the context of God sending messengers to humanity. However, Abboud contends that the verse is a response to Muhammad's opponents who claim that prophecy is exclusive only to angels and not to humans: "They thus seek to confirm Muhammad's claim of apostleship within his capacity as a human being and not within his capacity as a male messenger."[53] Moreover, the word *messengership* is used here in the verse, and based on the reading of Ibn Hazm, no one claims that

50. Tatari and von Stosch, *Mary in the Qur'an*, 311. For more on Maryam in comparative theology and a Muslim perspective, see Mona Siddiqui, ed., "Reflections on Mary," in *Christians, Muslims and Jesus* (Yale University Press, 2013).

51. See chapter 3.

52. Abboud, "'Idhan Maryam Nabiyya,'" 183–196.

53. Abboud, "'Idhan Maryam Nabiyya,'" 188.

Maryam was a messenger in the sense that she was sent to a particular community with a divine book. Instead, Maryam is a "prophet" because she received revelation directly from a divine messenger. For Abboud, Ibn Hazm (and al-Qurtubi) precede Muslim feminists by nine centuries in arguing against androcentric readings of the Qur'an.

Abboud also engages in her own reading of the text, where she sees that Maryam was an inspiration and model for Muhammad and the early Muslim community. She argues that Maryam has signs of a prophet such as "being accepted to serve in the temple, her purity and sinlessness (*'isma*), her righteous upbringing and miraculous sustenance, the angelic annunciation from God (*al-bishara*), and her being impregnated by the Holy Spirit *(min ruhina)*."[54] Meccan verses of the Qur'an repeat the narrative of messengers sent to their people, scorned and rejected but finally vindicated by God. Maryam fits a similar trope in that she was given a divine message and brought it to her people, but they rejected it, leading to the miracle of 'Isa's speech. As Abboud argues, "Like Muhammad, Maryam received a divine message delivered to her personally by means of the appearance of an angelic being. Like Muhammad, Maryam was abandoned and slandered by her own people because of this divine choosing of her for a special task. Like Muhammad and his followers, she experienced fear, hunger, thirst, and insecurity. Then, miraculously God vindicated her before those who ridiculed her, exemplifying the end that the rejected Muhammad waited for and anticipated."[55] For Abboud, Muhammad identified more with Maryam than he did with Jesus, as there are fuller narratives regarding her spiritual story and conflict with her people. Such a claim is not "farfetched," as there were strong Arab women in Muhammad's life and in the Arabian context, such as his first wife, Khadija, who arranged his religious consultations with the Christian priest Waraqa b. Nawfal when Muhammad was attempting to discern the first Qur'anic

54. Abboud, "'Idhan Maryam Nabiyya,'" 190.

55. Abboud, "'Idhan Maryam Nabiyya,'" 191.

revelations. Similar to Madigan, Abboud sees an analogy between Maryam and Muhammad in that they both carried the "word," with Maryam carrying ʿIsa and Muhammad the Qur'an. Abboud concludes by contending that the question of Maryam being a prophet and model for Muhammad could help present the "essentially egalitarian Islamic vision (ethical and spiritual) between the sexes" and serve as a way to counter "hierarchically" discriminatory social structures.[56] Moreover, Muhammad's identification with Maryam could help with Christian-Muslim dialogue and bring women together from each tradition in a "spirit of mutual understanding."[57]

Feminist engagements continue in Jerusha T. Rhodes's *Divine Words, Female Voices*.[58] In the introduction, she speaks about "poisoned wells" as an analogy to describe discussions around "Muslim women, egalitarianism, and Islamic feminism." On one side, Western feminists' critiques of Islam often position themselves in a place of cultural superiority and perpetuate negative stereotypes of Islam and Muslims. They further overlook the voices of Muslim women and consider the "well" of Islam as devoid of egalitarian possibilities. Muslim women are thus put in the difficult task of "drinking from the well" of their tradition, even while others may consider it to be harmful. On the other side, the well has been poisoned by "patriarchy and androcentrism" or "male dominance and male normativity" within the Islamic tradition.[59] The well has been poisoned in the sense that it can "often stifle—if not prevent—deep conversations and informed solidarity among women across religious traditions."[60] Rhodes, therefore, proposes a "Muslima"

56. Abboud, "'Idhan Maryam Nabiyya,'" 193.

57. Abboud, "'Idhan Maryam Nabiyya,'" 193.

58. Jerusha Tanner Lamptey, *Divine Words, Female Voices: Muslima Explorations in Comparative Feminist Theology* (Oxford University Press, 2018).

59. Lamptey, *Divine Words, Female Voices*, 2.

60. Lamptey, *Divine Words, Female Voices*, 2.

theology[61] that centers on Muslim women's voices, interreligious feminist engagement, and comparative theological exploration, especially between Christian and Muslim women.

Such an approach becomes evident in her comparison between Maryam and Muhammad, which she devotes an entire chapter to: "Bearers of the Words: Muhammad and Mary as Feminist Exemplars." In the chapter, Rhodes engages with Christian feminists' works on Mary to better understand the role of Muhammad as a model and example for all Muslims. Just as many Christian feminists challenge the role of Mary in supporting and enforcing patriarchal norms and androcentrism, Rhodes is critical of attempts to do the same with Muhammad as a "patriarchal exemplar." For instance, while Christian feminist scholars center the "femaleness" of Mary, Rhodes is explicit in emphasizing the "maleness" of Muhammad and how that could be a potential bridge or barrier to emulating the prophet. Rhodes further draws a connection between Muhammad and Mary in that they are both "intermediaries—even mediators—of the divine revelation."[62] Mary is "theological and literal 'womb' for Jesus" in the same way Muhammad is sent as a "mercy," which is derived from the same Arabic root (*r-h-m*) as the word *womb* (*rahm*). Moreover, the Prophet Muhammad's "virginal conception of the Qur'an is theologically parallel to that of Mary"[63] in that he was *ummi*, or could not read or write. Similarly, Maryam was a virgin and did not have a male partner but was still able to miraculously produce a child. Rhodes is thus able to use Maryam to construct a modern Muslim feminist theology and better understand Muhammad's role as a model and exemplar.[64]

61. See Jerusha Tanner Lamptey, *Never Wholly Other: A Muslima Theology of Religious Pluralism* (Oxford University Press, 2014).

62. Lamptey, *Never Wholly Other*, 140.

63. Lamptey, *Never Wholly Other*, 145.

64. For an overview of modern Muslim feminist literature, see Miriam Cooke, "Modern and Contemporary Muslim Feminist Literature: An Overview," in *The Oxford Handbook of Islam and Women*, ed. Asma Afsaruddin (Oxford University Press, 2023), 549–568. For more on how women are treated within the academy

## Qur'anic Translation and Commentary

Another aspect of Maryam's reception in modern times appears in the proliferation of Qur'anic translations and commentaries. Classical Qur'anic commentary was primarily in Arabic and accessible to the scholarly elite who gave sermons and taught classes to the masses. In contemporary times, there is a push to make the Qur'an and Qur'anic commentary accessible to general audiences who may not know Arabic or have a seminary background. Moreover, we see the rise of women participating in the translation and commentary of the Qur'an and thus providing unique perspectives and interpretations of key Qur'anic verses and stories, especially those on Maryam.[65]

---

and Islamic studies, see Kecia Ali, *The Woman Question in Islamic Studies* (Princeton University Press, 2024). For more on how Hagar is a model for many modern Muslim women, especially Arab, South Asian, and Black women, see Amina Wadud, *Inside the Gender Jihad: Women's Reform in Islam* (Oneworld, 2006); Aziza Hibri, "Hagar on My Mind," in *Philosophy, Feminism, and Faith*, ed. Ruth E. Groenhoutt and Marya Bower (Indiana University Press, 2003), 198–210; Riffat Hasan, "Islamic Hagar and Her Family," in *Hagar, Sarah, and Their Children*, ed. Phyliss Trible and Letty M. Russel (Westminster John Knox, 2006). Hibba Abugideiri, "Hagar: A Historical Model for 'Gender Jihad,'" in *Daughters of Abraham: Feminist Thought in Judaism, Christianity, and Islam*, ed. Yvonne Y. Haddad and John L. Esposito (University Press of Florida, 2001); Aysha Hidayatullah, "Beyond Sarah and Hagar: Jewish and Muslim Reflections on Feminist Theology," in *Muslims and Jews in America Commonalities, Contentions, and Complexities*, ed. R. Aslan and A. J. Hahn Tapper (Palgrave Macmillan, 2011). For more on Maryam in gender and sexuality, see H. Lamya, *Hijab Butch Blues: A Memoir* (The Dial Press, 2023).

65. For more on modern women's interpretation of the Qur'an, see Hadia Mubarak, "Women's Contemporary Readings of the Qur'an," in *The Routledge Companion to the Qur'an*, ed. George Archer, Maria Dakake, and Daniel Madigan (Routledge, 2022), 319–333; Hidayet Aydar and Mehmet Atalay, "Female Scholars of Qur'anic Exegesis in the History of Islam," *Journal of Theology Faculty of Bülent Ecevit University* 1, no. 2 (2014): 1–34. For more on contemporary efforts toward translation, see Johanna Pink, "Translation," in *The Routledge Companion to the Qur'an*, ed. George Archer, Maria Dakake, and Daniel Madigan (Routledge, 2022), 364–376. For more on women translations, see Najlaa R. Aldeeb, "Feminist Strategies in Qur'an Translations: A Comparative Study of the Sublime Quran and Saheeh International," *International Journal of Linguistics, Literature and Translation* 6, no. 1 (2023): 10–19. For more on women and the Qur'anic commentary (*tafsir*) tradition, see Shuruq Naguib, "Bint

For instance, Maria Dakake, in *The Study Qur'an*, comments on the chapter of Maryam and provides her own interpretation of classical debates while engaging with major exegeses.[66] In the discussion regarding Maryam's wish that she "died before this," Dakake understands that this statement is a result of the "onset of difficulties she now faced as a woman giving birth to a child alone, without a husband, including both the physical pain of labor and embarrassment about what people would think of her."[67] Dakake thus reconciles both opinions that her call was a result of her labor pain and her concern about facing her people. She also adds that commentators note that her longing for death should not be understood as a "lacked patience, contentment, or trust in God."[68] Rather, the great Qur'anic commentator al-Razi "observes that longing for death is often the response of the righteous to suffering, as they refuse to abandon their moral or spiritual duties, but are nonetheless fearful of or saddened by the consequences that may result."[69] Al-Razi gives the example of 'Ali, the cousin of the Prophet and fourth caliph, who makes a similar statement before the Battle of the Camel, the opening battle of the first Muslim civil war. In regard to Maryam's call that she wished to be "utterly forgotten," Dakake provides a spiritual commentary: "Mary's statement can be understood as expressing the ultimate victory against the worldly ego, for it indicates that she wished not only to withdraw from and forget

al-Shati''s Approach to *tafsir*: An Egyptian Exegete's Journey from Hermeneutics to Humanity," *Journal of Qur'anic Studies* 17, no. 1 (2015): 45–84.

66. As Seyyed Hossein Nasr notes in the introduction, "Ours is therefore a new commentary that is nonetheless based completely on traditional Islamic thought and the earlier commentary traditions." Seyyed Hossein Nasr, *The Study Quran: A New Translation and Commentary* (HarperOne 2015), xliv. Nasir also explains that *The Study Qur'an* was meant to complement *The HarperCollins Study Bible*.

67. Dakake, *The Study Qur'an*, 770.

68. Dakake, *The Study Qur'an*, 770.

69. Dakake, *The Study Qur'an*, 770.

the world, but also to utterly forgotten by it."[70] Maryam did not desire worldly fame and recognition, and her ability to detach from the world gave her the capacity to overcome the present challenge and obstacle.

Moreover, Dakake references mystical commentaries that emphasize a spiritual interpretation of the story. For instance, verse 19:16 speaks of Maryam withdrawing from her family "to an eastern place." After going through the various commentaries that attempt to identify the physical location, Dakake adds that others "refer to Mary's spiritual withdrawal from the realm of existent being . . . in order to enter the realm of the Spirit . . . where she would witness and encounter the Divine and the 'eternal breath of union.'" She continues that "the present verse can be understood to mean that one cannot encounter the spiritual dimension of reality until one withdraws from all worldly things that distract one from the remember of God."[71] Maryam's withdrawal should not only be understood in historical and geographical terms but also spiritual ones in that it reflects mystical concepts of solitude and isolation (*khalwa*). Once Maryam is alone, she must only rely on God, his power and blessings. Another example is verse 19:26, "So eat and drink," which once again not only should be interpreted literally but is also "symbolic of God's love and concern for her."[72] God loved Maryam and thus provided her with nourishment when she was in need and distress.

Last, Dakake has an ecumenical spirit in that she stresses that Maryam "represents a unique point of connection between Islam, Judaism and Christianity."[73] She was born into a priestly Jewish family that was dedicated to the service of the temple, but she was also the mother of Jesus, who played the foundational role in Christianity. Maryam continues to be important in Islam, with her story recounted in different places, and plays a "significant role in certain forms of Islamic

70. Dakake, *The Study Qur'an*, 770.

71. Dakake, *The Study Qur'an*, 768.

72. Dakake, *The Study Qur'an*, 770.

73. Dakake, *The Study Qur'an*, 763.

piety."[74] Dakake cites the famous story of the Muslims in Abyssinia reciting the chapter of Maryam after Negus requested that they recite from the Qur'an. As a result, "Negus and the religious leaders of his court began to weep profusely and refused to hand over the Muslims, indicating that the religious teachings of the Qur'an were deeply related to those of the Christian faith."[75] Similar to other modern writers, Dakake sees Maryam as representing a potential bridge among various religions and playing a special role in Christian-Muslim relations.[76]

## Shared Visions of Maryam

While Maryam appears in the writings of scholars, theologians, and exegeses, she also appears in the visions of the masses. The concepts of miracles and mysticism continue into the modern period and take on a new interfaith spirit. These visions often represent the voice of the masses and their hopes and aspirations as they contend with the struggles and challenges of their daily lives.[77] In many ways, they represent a folk religion that emerges from the grassroots rather than the clergy and religious elite and represent a decentralized form of spirituality.

For instance, there was a shared vision of Mary in 1968 in Cairo that was reportedly seen by thousands of Christians and Muslims. Muslim workmen heard a disturbance in the street and came out to

---

74. Dakake, *The Study Qur'an*, 764

75. Dakake, *The Study Qur'an*, 764.

76. See also *The Sublime Quran*, trans. Laleh Bakhtiar (Kazi Publications, 2007), http://islamicworld.com. Bakhtiar's translation is unique since it highlights when the feminine second-person pronouns are used, which is significant in the story of Maryam, as God and Gabriel/Jibril communicate directly to her. Bakhtiar's translation choice thus highlights the immediate and intimate connection between Maryam and the divine messengers.

77. Willy Jansen, "Visions of Mary in the Middle East: Gender and the Power of a Symbol," in *Gender, Religion and Change in the Middle East: Two Hundred Years of History*, ed. Inger Marie Okkenhaug and Ingvild Flaskerud (Bloomsbury, 2005): 137–154.

see a moving light on the dome of a Coptic church and thought it was a woman who had climbed to the roof to commit suicide. They cried out to her to be careful, but somebody began to yell that it was the Virgin Mary. Some reports even have her holding an olive branch as a sign of peace and appearing in the town of Zeitun, which means *olives.*[78] The various reports affirm that she was silent and seemed to be in a state of prayer, allowing those who witnessed her to "project their own relation with God and, more specifically, to identify with her."[79] While she reportedly appeared above a Coptic church, she did not say anything explicitly affirming Christian or Muslim creed, allowing her to be accepted by both populations. For instance, some witnessed that Mary stood silently with the baby Jesus/'Isa in her hands, which for Christians represented Christ's humanity while for Muslims represented the birth story depicted in the chapter of Maryam in the Qur'an.[80]

That vision of Mary would appear on and off for two years and become an attraction not only for the Christian minority population but also for the Muslim majority as well. For instance, one of the Muslim bus drivers watching the light held up to Mary a seriously injured finger that needed amputation, and the next day, his doctor found a complete recovery. In another story, a Muslim named Muhammad Zaki was suffering from angina, or coronary artery disease, and went to Zeitun to pray to God to cure him. Once he got home, "he had another attack and, while he was in bed, he again asked God to cure him. At that point, he heard the door of his bedroom open, and saw a woman who was surrounded with light. She came up to him and reassured him. He began to recite the verses from the Koran that mention how Mary was

78. Sandrine Keriakos, "Apparitions of the Virgin in Egypt: Improving Relations Between Copts and Muslims?" in *Sharing Sacred Spaces in the Mediterranean*, ed. Dionigi Albera and Maria Couroucli (Indiana University Press, 2012), 174–201.

79. Keriakos, "Apparitions of the Virgin in Egypt," 191.

80. Maura Hearden, "Lessons from Zeitoun: A Marian Proposal for Christian-Muslim Dialogue," *Journal of Ecumenical Studies* 47, no. 3 (2012), 416.

chosen by God. The next day, he was better."[81] This last story incorporates Qur'anic verses that combine Christian and Muslim experiences and scriptures. Such stories circulated among the Muslim populations and attested to the authenticity of the apparitions since Muslims were seen as neutral and credible sources not associated with the church over which she appeared.

The shared vision was seen as part of Mary's/Maryam's favor of Egypt and her desire to see peaceful relations between Christians and Muslims, dating back to the premodern period. For instance, the Abbasid caliph al-Ma'mun (r. 813–833) had ordered the destruction of all the churches in Egypt, but the priest in charge asked for a four-day stay of execution. During that period, the Virgin reportedly appeared to the caliph and softened his heart. All the churches in the country were thus spared.[82] Moreover, the vision occurred right after the 1967 war between Egypt and Israel, which Egypt lost, leading to national sadness and turmoil. The vision of Mary seemed to comfort the population and demonstrate that God's mercy and care were descending on them.[83] The 1967 war would precipitate a religious revival, and there was a hope that both Christians and Muslims would become united in a national and patriotic struggle for Egypt's postcolonial liberation.[84]

The vision further appeared at a time when gender roles were being renegotiated and women began to play a more active role within Egyptian society. Mary/Maryam's public and visible appearance seemed

81. Keriakos, "Apparitions of the Virgin in Egypt," 185.

82. Keriakos, "Apparitions of the Virgin in Egypt," 176.

83. Donald A. Westbrook, "Our Lady of Zeitoun (1968–1971) Egyptian Mariophanies in Historical, Interfaith, and Ecumenical Context," *Nova Religio: The Journal of Alternative and Emergent Religions* 21, no. 2 (2017): 85–99.

84. Hearden, "Lessons from Zeitoun," 426.

to support Egyptian women in their attempts to play a more public and visible role.[85]

## Conclusion

Maryam continues into the modern period with references to the Qur'an, miracles, and mysticism. However, we see a unique emphasis on her identity as a woman, have begun to see women scholars write about her, and witness a new ecumenical and interfaith spirit. Maryam is not only a model of faith and piety but also a bridge to Christianity and a way to live in a more peaceful and just world. Whether through pilgrimage sites, statements, or visions, Maryam has become a symbol of shared devotion and spirituality.

85. For a critical appraisal of these apparitions and how they fit within the larger Egyptian religious landscape, see Angie Heo, "The Virgin Between Christianity and Islam: Sainthood, Media, and Modernity in Egypt," *Journal of the American Academy of Religion* 81, no. 4 (2013): 1117–1138.

# Conclusion

To conclude, I want to end with how Maryam remains important and relevant today.

First, Maryam is a bridge figure and personality shared between Christianity and Islam, the two largest world religions. Recent decades have seen world conflicts, from the Holy Lands to the Balkans, where religion is fundamental, as it constructs identities, helps shape narratives, and even instigates war. Personally, I was a teenager during the Bosnian war and was in my second year of college (in Washington, DC) when 9/11 occurred. Global religious conflict dominated my upbringing and influenced a generation to think of ways to bring people together to challenge xenophobia, religious misunderstanding, and war. Even from a very early period, Maryam allowed Muslims to connect with Christians in Ethiopia and to Christian delegations in Medina. She has been an interfaith symbol throughout Islamic history, from miracles to modest dress. More scholarship, activism, and forums should develop around Maryam to think of ways in which she can help bring Christians and Muslims (and people of all faiths) together on common visions, projects, and goals.

With regard to Islam specifically, Maryam allows us to see the religion through a different prism than is traditionally provided. Islam is often presented through its rituals (the five pillars), articles of faith, or contemporary politics. In scriptural studies, Islam is presented through Abraham/Ibrahim, the spiritual patriarch who connects Judaism, Christianity, and Islam. While these frames are relevant and important, Maryam provides a new lens that sheds light on unique aspects of the faith that would have been overlooked otherwise. Maryam lets us see better how Islamic tradition views scripture, women, theology, mysticism, art, and ecumenical relations. Maryam touches almost all aspects of Islam and appears in nearly every major debate.

Second, Maryam allows us to access scripture. Our modern lives appear so far removed from the time of the Bible and Qur'an and, at times, even strange to and at odds with our modern values and sensibilities. The Qur'an and hadith are in classical Arabic, which is often hard for Arabs, let alone non-Arabic speakers, to understand and comprehend. However, the scriptural sources provide a coherent story of Maryam that is relatable to people across time and space. The Qur'an even has a chapter named after Maryam with a distinct rhyme scheme, message, and theme. Whether it be her birth, miracles, or struggles, people have connected with her in various ways and find inspiration in her model and example. Maryam allows us to better access scripture and understand why it continues to be relevant to religious, spiritual, and academic communities.

Third, Maryam teaches us about spirituality and the miraculous. The quest to better understand who we are in relationship to the world around us is a universal theme shared across cultures and space. People seek meaning in their lives and look to history for inspiration, guidance, and wisdom. Maryam endures because she has influenced and shaped the lives of countless people through her resolute faith, willingness to accept her fate and mission, and struggle to bring what was within her into the world. Moreover, while we may be skeptical about miracles in the modern world, they are everywhere in our fiction and imagination. Miracles are ever present in the story of Maryam, from her pregnancy to being provided fruits out of season. Miracles allow us to think of the transcendent and incredible and beyond the mundane. They inspire, challenge, and motivate us to think of ways the world could be different and transformative. They also give us hope that life can succeed despite the remarkable obstacles and odds.

Last, Maryam endures because she reminds us of the concept of motherhood, especially regarding pregnancy and labor. The Qur'an speaks about her pregnancy, labor, and the eventual birth of her child, 'Isa, and contains verses that allude to motherhood and birth. Muslim memory has been influenced by this portrayal, and the concept of motherhood is seen throughout Islamic history in poetry and art. It makes us recognize that we all come from a womb, and there could never be 'Isa without Maryam. It is why Mother's Day is one of the most popular holidays and why many of us remain loyal to our mothers despite the various challenges and setbacks. Regardless of our family conflicts, we realize and appreciate the pain, struggle, and labor that our mothers went through and honor their efforts to bring us into existence. This labor is not only physical but also a spiritual act and a means to connect to others and the transcendent.

In particular, the idea of pregnancy and labor should not only be seen as exclusively female but can also be seen in a more universal light, even for those who are not women and do not have children. We saw, in chapter 4, how the poetry of Rumi speaks about pregnancy in a more universal sense, for example. We all have something inside of us that is growing, developing, and forming, whether it is an idea, a project, or a child. The incubation period may take months or even years, and we struggle to give birth. However, once we do, the transformation can be immense and even life-changing for us and those around us. Maryam allows us to reflect on what we have inside us and how it can potentially change the world.

# ACKNOWLEDGMENTS

As I finish this book, I feel a sense of excitement and jubilation. I have been "pregnant" with this book for years as my research delved into how medieval scholars engaged in prophetic literature and Arabic and biblical sources. This niche research led me to write a more general book on biblical and Qur'anic figures that could engage academic and popular audiences. Through its writing, I was fascinated by the story of Maryam and how it had not been fully told or explained. While there have been several books on Abraham, there were not as many on Maryam and her role in history, the modern period, and contemporary relations. Seeing an idea come to life, from a proposal to a draft to an actual book, is remarkable and extraordinary. It is almost like seeing a tree grow to fruition or raising a child to maturity.

But I also feel a sense of sadness and uncertainty. Maryam was a companion and guide to me for the last several years. I would wake up at the crack of dawn almost every day and write about her story, history, and memory. She took me places I would never have gone if I had stayed within my academic niche or discipline. Through Maryam, I had the opportunity to see connections in the Qur'an that I hadn't seen before, such as those regarding labor, birth, and childrearing. I learned how early Muslims used her as an interfaith symbol and how the Prophet Muhammad praised her and other Arab women. I saw how Muslim theologians debated over her status, with some arguing that she was a prophet and the best woman of all time. I engaged in Sufi literature and poetry that used her as a model of spirituality and reliance on God. I appreciated how she was incorporated into Islamic art and became a spiritual matriarch for dynasties. I saw how Maryam flourished in modernity as an ecumenical symbol and inspiration for female leadership and spirituality. Now that this book is done, I am unsure what my mornings will look like and what I will research and write. I will miss Maryam's mentorship, friendship, and companionship. Nonetheless, her legacy will forever live within me wherever I go and whatever I write.

However, Maryam has opened new doors for me that I hope to walk through. She has led me to other historical Muslim female figures such as Umm Salama and Rabi'a al-'Adawiyya. She has made me better appreciate shared biblical and Qur'anic figures such as Abraham/Ibrahim and Moses/Musa. She has led me to explore new concepts such as love and interfaith relations. She made me form new relationships and partnerships with nonprofit organizations, scholars, and community members. I don't know where these doors and opportunities will take me, but I know I have Maryam to thank and appreciate.

I further want to thank the Maryams in my life: my wife, Rehenuma Asmi; my mother, Tanveer Mirza; and my sisters, Fatima, Asma, and Sana Mirza. Moreover, I want to thank my Zakariyya—my dad, M. Yaqub Mirza—for his support and encouragement.

Emily King was the editor who first solicited this project and was "the voice from below" that gave me the confidence and motivation to put it together. Adam Bursi was the "midwife" who helped "deliver" the book and make it come into the world. John Kaltner provided helpful feedback on an earlier version of this manuscript and introduced me to how shared figures could help teach Islam and interreligious relations. Martin Nguyen has been a constant friend and guide and provided insightful comments on earlier drafts. Celene Ibrahim also made comments, and her work on women in the Qur'an has been inspiring. Ermin Sinanovic and the Center for Islam in the Contemporary World provided the encouragement and research support to make the work become a reality.

In the end, I want to thank you, the reader, for picking up and engaging this book. While the author writes, it is the reader, like Gabriel/Jibril, who breathes their spirit into it and makes it alive and meaningful. A story remains untold if nobody can hear, react, and engage. Your finding this book worthy of your time is a profound honor to me and makes me feel that it was worth writing despite the various challenges and obstacles. I hope to meet many of you someday and learn how Maryam impacted your life, religious practice, and spiritual journey.

# BIBLIOGRAPHY


Abbas, Shemeem Burney. *The Female Voice in Sufi Ritual: Devotional Practices of Pakistan and India*. University of Texas Press, 2002.

Abboud, Hosn. *Mary in the Qur'an: A Literary Reading*. Routledge / Taylor and Francis, 2014.

———. "'Idhan Maryam Nabiyya' ['Hence Maryam Is a Prophetess']: Muslim Classical Exegetes and Women's Receptiveness to God's Verbal Inspiration." In *Mariam, the Magdalen, and the Mother*, edited by Deirdre Joy Good. Indiana University Press, 2005.

———. "Is Mary Important for Herself or for Being the Mother of Christ in the Holy Qur'an?" *Al-Raida* 125 (2009): 26–36.

Abdel Haleem, M. A. S. "Chapter Maryam (19): Providing Muhammad with Comfort." *Journal of Qur'anic Studies* 22, no. 2 (2020): 62–81.

Abdel Naby, Heba Mahmoud Saad, and Heba Magdy. "The Representation of Virgin Mary in Islamic Art During the Ayyubid Dynasty (12th–13th Century)." *International Journal of History and Cultural Studies (IJHCS)* 4, no. 4 (2018): 20–41.

Abi Ja'far Muhammad b. al-Hasan al-Tusi. *al-Tibyan fi tafsir al-*Qur'an, edited by Ahmad Habib Qasir al-'Amili. Dar Ihya' al-Turath al-'Arabi, 1409/1989.

Abou El Fadl, Khaled. "Islamic Law and Muslim Minorities: The Juristic Discourse on Muslim Minorities from the Second/Eighth to the Eleventh/Seventeenth Centuries." *Islamic Law and Society* 1, no. 2 (1994): 141–187.

———. "Legal Debates on Muslim Minorities: Between Rejection and Accommodation." *Journal of Religious Ethics* 22, no. 1 (1994): 127–162.

Abugideiri, Hibba. "Hagar: A Historical Model for 'Gender Jihad.'" In *Daughters of Abraham: Feminist Thought in Judaism, Christianity, and Islam*, edited by Yvonne Y. Haddad and John L. Esposito. University Press of Florida, 2001.

Akkad, Moustafa, director. *The Message*. Trancas, 1976.

Aldeeb Abu-Sahlieh, Sami A. "The Islamic Conception of Migration." *International Migration Review* 30, no. 1 (1996): 37–57.

Aldeeeb, Najlaa R. "Feminist Strategies in Qur'ān Translations: A Comparative Study of the Sublime Quran and Saheeh International." *International Journal of Linguistics, Literature and Translation* 6 (2023): 10–19.

Aldin, Andrew F. "Sources of Moral Obligation to Non-Muslims in the 'Jurisprudence of Muslim Minorities' (Fiqh al-Aqalliyyat) Discourse." *Islamic Law and Society* 16, no. 1 (2009): 34–94.

Alhassen, Leyla Ozgur. *Quranic Stories: God, Revelation and the Audience.* Edinburgh University Press, 2021.

———. "A Structural Analysis of Surat Maryam, Verses 1–58." *Journal of Qur'anic Studies* 18, no. 1 (2016): 97–109.

Ali, Fariha. "Aniconism in Islam." *al-Salihat* 1, no. 2 (2022): 1–16.

Ali, Kecia. "Destabilizing Gender, Reproducing Maternity: Mary in the Qur'ān." *Journal of the International Qur'anic Studies Association* 2 (2017): 89–109.

Ali, Kecia. *The Woman Question in Islamic Studies.* Princeton University Press, 2024.

Al-Alwani, Taha Jaber. "'Fatwa' Concerning the United States Supreme Courtroom Frieze." *Journal of Law and Religion* 15, no. 1/2 (2000–2001): 1–28.

Al-Asqalani, Ibn Hajar. *Fath al-bari bi-sharh al-Bukhari*, edited by Muhammad Fu'ad 'Abd al-Baqi and Muhibb al-Din al-Katib. al-Maktaba al-Salafiyya, 1911.

Al-Bukhari. *Sahih al-Bukhari.* Dar Ibn Kathir, 2002.

Al-Faruqi, Isma'il. *The Arts of Islamic Civilization.* International Institute of Islamic Thought, 2013.

Al-Khajuri, Muhammad Baqir. *al-Khasa'is al-Fatimiyya.* al-Sharif al-Radi, 1959.

Al-Qurtubi, Muhammad b. Ahmad. *al-Jami' li-ahkam al-Qur'an: wa'l-mubayyin li-ma tadammanahu min al-sunna wa-ay al-Furqan*, edited by 'Abd Allah b. 'Abd al-Muhsin al-Turki and Muhammad Ridwan 'Irqsusi. 24 vols. Mu'assasat al-Risala, 2006.

Al-Razi, Fakhr al-Din. *al-Tafsir al-Kabir*, edited by Sayyid 'Umran. 32 vols. Dar al-Hadith, 2012.

al-Sabuni, Nur al-Din. *An Introduction to Islamic Theology (al-Bidayah fi usul al-din).* Translated and edited by Faraz Khan. Zaytuna Institute, 2020.

Al-Tabari, Abu Ja'far Muhammad b. Jarir. *Jami' al-bayan fi tafsir al-Qur'an*, edited by 'Abd Allah b. 'Abd al-Muhsin al-Turki. 26 vols. Dar al-Hijr, 2001.

Al-Tirmidhi, Muhammad b. 'Isa. *al-Jami' al-kabir*, edited by Bashshar 'Awwad Ma'ruf. 6 vols. Dar al-Gharb al-Islami, 1996.

Al-Tusi, Abi Ja'far Muhammad b al-Hasan. *al-Tibyan fi tafsir al-Qur'an*, edited by Ahmad Habib Qasir al-'Amili. Dar Ihya' al-Turath al-'Arabi, 1409/1989.

Amanullah, Muhammad. "Debate over the Karamah of Allah's Friends." *Arab Law Quarterly* 18, no. 3 (2003): 365–374.

Azad, Arezou. "Female Mystics in Mediaeval Islam: The Quiet Legacy." *Journal of the Economic and Social History of the Orient* 56 (2013): 53–88.

Azadibougar, Omid, and Simon Patton. "Coleman Barks' Versions of Rumi in the USA." *Translation and Literature* 24, no. 2 (2015): 172–189.

Bahrani, Shahriar, dir. *Maryam Moghaddas*. Sima Film WN Media, 2000.

Bakker, Freek L. "The Image of Muhammad in *The Message*, the First and Only Feature Film About the Prophet of Islam." *Islam and Christian–Muslim Relations* 17, no. 1 (2006): 77–92.

Bakhos, Carol. *The Family of Abraham: Jewish, Christian, and Muslim Interpretations*. Harvard University Press, 2014.

Barks, Coleman, trans. *The Essential Rumi*. HarperOne, 2004.

Barlas, Asma. "The Qur'an and Hermeneutics: Reading the Qur'an's Opposition to Patriarchy." *Journal of Qur'anic Studies* 3, no. 2 (2001): 15–38.

Bezirgan, Basima Qattan, and Elizabeth Warnock Fernea, eds. *Middle Eastern Women Speak*. University of Texas Press, 1977.

Blair, Sheila S., and Jonathan M. Bloom. "The Mirage of Islamic Art: Reflections on the Study of an Unwieldy Field." *Art Bulletin* 85, no. 1 (2003): 152–184.

Blecher, Joel. *Said the Prophet of God: Hadith Commentary Across a Millennium*. University of California Press, 2017.

Blecher, Joel, and Stefanie Brinkmann, eds. *Hadith Commentary: Continuity and Change*. Edinburgh University Press, 2023.

Bop, Codou. "Roles and the Position of Women in Sufi Brotherhoods in Senegal." *Journal of the American Academy of Religion* 73, no. 4 (December 2005): 1099–1119.

Bowen, Donna Lee. "Infanticide." In *Encyclopaedia of the Qur'ān*, edited by Jane Dammen McAuliffe. E. J. Brill, 2021.

———. "Birth." In *Encyclopaedia of the Qur'ān*, edited by Jane Dammen McAuliffe. E. J. Brill, 2021.

Brown, Jonathan A. C. *Hadith: Muhammad's Legacy in the Medieval and Modern World*. Oneworld, 2009.

———. "Faithful Dissenters: Sunni Skepticism About the Miracles of Saints." *Journal of Sufi Studies* 1 (2012): 123–168.

Burney, Shemeem Abbas. *The Female Voice in Sufi Ritual: Devotional Practices of Pakistan and India*. University of Texas Press, 2002.

Calis, Halim. "Mary's Prophethood Reassessed: Overlooked Medieval Islamic Perspectives in Contemporary Scholarship." *Religions* 15 (2024): 1–12.

Carey, Moya, and Margaret S. Graves. "Introduction: the Historiography of Islamic Art and Architecture, 2012." *Journal of Art Historiography* 6 (2012): 1–15.

Carroll, Donal. *Mary's House: the Extraordinary Story Behind the Discovery of the House Where the Virgin Mary Lived and Died*. Christian Classics, 2002.

Chittick, William, and Jalal al-Din Rumi. *The Sufi Path of Love: The Spiritual Teachings of Rumi*. State University of New York Press, 1983.

Cooke, Miriam. "Modern and Contemporary Muslim Feminist Literature: An Overview." In *The Oxford Handbook of Islam and Women*, edited by Asma Afsaruddin. Oxford University Press, 2023.

Cornell, Rkia. *Early Sufi Women: Dhikr an-niswa al-muta'abbidat as-Sufiyyat*. Translated by Rkia Cornell. Fons Vitae, 1999.

———. *Rabi'a from Narrative to Myth: The Many Faces of Islam's Most Famous Woman Saint, Rabi'a al-'Adawiyya*. Oneworld Academic, 2019.

Creswell, K. A. C. "The Ka'ba in A.D. 608." *Archaeologia: or Miscellaneous Tracts Relating to Antiquity* 94 (1951): 97–102.

Dakake, Maria. "'Guest of the Inmost Heart': Conceptions of the Divine Beloved Among Early Sufi Women." *Journal of Comparative Islamic Studies* 3, no. 1 (2007): 75–92.

———. "Re-reading the Quranic Maryam as a Mystic in Nusrat Amin's Makhzan-i 'irfan." In *Islamic Thought and the Art of Translation: Texts and Studies in Honor of William C. Chittick and Sachiko Murata*, edited by Mohammed Rustom. Brill, 2023.

———. "Walking upon the Path of God like Men?: Women and the Feminine in the Islamic Mystical Tradition." *Sophia: A Journal of Traditional Studies* 8, no. 2 (2002): 132–142.

Diaz, Marta Dominguez. *Women in Sufism: Female Religiosities in a Transnational Order*. Routledge, 2015.

Elias, Jamal. "The Female and Feminine in Islamic Mysticism." *The Muslim World* 78 (1988): 209–224.

Ellis, Kail, ed. *Nostra Aetate, Non-Christian Religions, and Interfaith Relations*. Palgrave Macmillan, 2021.

Ellul, Joseph. "The Issue of Muslim-Christian Dialogue 'Nostra Aetate' Revisited." *Angelicum* 84, no. 2 (2007): 361–381.

El-Zein, Amira. "Spiritual Consumption in the United States: The Rumi Phenomenon." *Islam Christian-Muslim Relations* 11, no. 1 (2000): 81–95.

Ernst, Carl. *Sufism: An Introduction to the Mystical Tradition of Islam.* Shambhala, 2011.

Esin, Emel. "The Qur'anic Verses and the Hadith as Sources of Inspiration in Islamic Art." In *Islamic Art: Common Principles, Forms and Themes,* edited by Ahmad Muhammad 'Isaa and Tahsin Omer Tahaoglu. Dar al-Fikr, 1989.

Ettinghausen, Richard, Sheila Blair, and Oleg Grabar. *The Art and Architecture of Islam, 650–1250.* Yale University Press, 1994.

———. "Islam and Art." *Studia Islamica* 37 (1973): 81–109.

Feiler, Bruce S. *Abraham: A Journey to the Heart of Three Faiths.* W. Morrow, 2002.

Fernea, Elizabeth Warnock, and Basima Qattan Bezirgan, eds. *Middle Eastern Women Speak.* University of Texas Press, 1977.

Fierro, Maribel. "The Polemic About the *karamat al-awliya'* and the Development of Sufism in al-Andalus." *Bulletin of the School of Oriental and African Studies, University of London* 55, no. 2 (1992): 236–249.

———. "Women as Prophets." In *Writing the Feminine: Women in Arab Sources,* edited by Randi Deguilhem and Manuela Marín. I. B. Tauris, 2002.

Flood, Finbarr Barry. "Idol-Breaking as Image-Making in the 'Islamic State.'" *Religion and Society: Advances in Research* 7 (2016): 116–138.

———. "From Prophet to Postmodernism? New World Orders and the End of Islamic Art." In *Making Art History: A Changing Discipline and Its Institutions,* edited by Elizabeth Mansfield. Routledge, 2007.

Furlanetto, Elena. "The Rumi Phenomenon Between Orientalism and Cosmopolitanism: The Case of Elif Shafak's *The Forty Rules of Love.*" *European Journal of English Studies* 17, no. 2 (2013): 201–213.

George-Tvrtkovič, Rita. *Christians, Muslims, and Mary: A History.* Paulist Press, 2018.

Giladi, Avner. "Some Observations on Infanticide in Medieval Muslim Society." *International Journal of Middle East Studies* 22 (1990): 185–200.

Gökkir, Bilal. "Form and Structure of Sura Maryam—A Study from Unity of Sura Perspective," *Süleyman Demirel Üniversitesi İlahiyat Fakültesi Dergisi* 16, no. 1 (2006): 1–16.

Grabar, Oleg. "From the Icon to Aniconism: Islam and the Image." *Museum International* 218, no. 55 (2003): 46–53.

———. "Islam and Iconoclasm." In *Early Islamic Art, 650–1100,* volume I of *Constructing the Study of Islamic Art,* edited by A. Bryer and J. Herrin. Ashgate, 2005.

Grabar, Oleg, ed. "Islamic Attitudes Towards Arts." In *The Formation of Islamic Art*. Yale University Press, 1987.

Haleem, M. A. S. Abdel, trans. *The Qur'an*. Oxford University Press, 2008.

Hasan, Riffat. "Islamic Hagar and Her Family." In *Hagar, Sarah, and Their Children*, edited by Phyllis Trible and Letty M. Russell. Westminster John Knox, 2006.

Hearden, Maura. "Lessons from Zeitoun: A Marian Proposal for Christian-Muslim Dialogue." *Journal of Ecumenical Studies* 47, no. 3 (2012): 409–426.

Helminski, Camille Adams. *Women of Sufism: A Hidden Treasure: Writings and Stories of Mystic Poets, Scholars and Saints*. Shambhala, 2003.

Heo, Angie. "The Virgin Between Christianity and Islam: Sainthood, Media, and Modernity in Egypt." *Journal of the American Academy of Religion* 81, no. 4 (2013): 1117–1138.

Hibri, Aziza. "Hagar on My Mind." In *Philosophy, Feminism, and Faith*, edited by Ruth E. Groenhout and Marya Bower. Indiana University Press, 2003.

Hidayatullah, Aysha. "Beyond Sarah and Hagar: Jewish and Muslim Reflections on Feminist Theology." In *Muslims and Jews in America: Commonalities, Contentions, and Complexities*, edited by R. Aslan and A. J. Hahn Tapper. Palgrave Macmillan, 2011.

Hidayet Aydar, and Mehmet Atalay. "Female Scholars of Qur'anic Exegesis in the History of Islam." *Journal of Theology Faculty of Bülent Ecevit University* 1, no. 2 (2014): 1–34.

Hillenbrand, Robert. "Oleg Grabar: the Scholarly Legacy." *Journal of Art Historiography* 6 (2012): 1–35.

Hoover, Jacqueline. "Mary/Maryam as a Prophet in the Islamic and Christian Traditions." In *Prophets in the Qur'an and the Bible*, edited by Sin-jong Paek and Sam Kim. Wipf and Stock, 2022.

Horsfjord, Vebjørn L. "A Common Word." In *Routledge Handbook on Christian-Muslim Relations*, edited by David Thomas. Routledge, 2018.

Huntington, Samuel. "The Clash of Civilizations?" *Foreign Affairs* 72, no. 3 (1993): 29.

———. *The Clash of Civilizations and the Remaking of World Order*. Simon and Schuster, 1996.

Ibn Abi al-'Izz, 'Ali b. 'Ali b. Muhammad. *Sharh al-'Aqidah al-Tahawiyya*, edited by 'Abd Allah b. al-Muhsin al-Turki and Shu'ayb al-Arna'ut. Mu'assasat al-Risalah, 1987.

Ibn Hazm, 'Ali b. Ahmad. *al-Ihkam fi usul al-ahkam*. 2 vols. Dar al-Kutub al-'Ilmiyya, 1985.

Ibn Hisham. *al-Sira al-Nabawiyya*, edited by 'Umar 'Abd al-Salam Tadmuri. 4 vols. Dar al-Kitab al-'Arabi, 1999.

Ibn Ishaq. *al-Sira al-Nabawiyya*, edited by Muhammad b. Ishaq b. Yasar. 2 vols. Dar al-Kutub al-'Ilmiyya, 2004.

Ibn Kathir. *Tafsir al-Qur'an al-'Azim*, edited by Sami Muhammad al-Salama. 8 vols. Dar Tayyiba, 1998.

Ibn Taymiyya. *al-Jawab al-sahih li-man baddala din al-Masiḥ*, edited by 'Ali b. Hasan b. Nasir, 'Abd al-'Aziz b. Ibrahim 'Askar, and Hamd b. Muhammad Hamdan. 7 vols. Dar al-'Asima, 1999.

Ibrahim, Celene. *Women and Gender in the Qur'an*. Oxford University Press, 2020.

Izzi Dien, Mawil Y., and P. E. Walker. "Wilaya." In *Encyclopaedia of Islam*, 2nd ed., edited by P. Bearman, Th. Bianquis, C. E. Bosworth, E. van Donzel, and W. P. Heinrichs. E. J. Brill, 2012.

Jansen, Willy. "Visions of Mary in the Middle East: Gender and the Power of a Symbol." In *Gender, Religion and Change in the Middle East: Two Hundred Years of History*, edited by Inger Marie Okkenhaug and Ingvild Flaskerud. Bloomsbury, 2005.

Kaltner, John, and Younus Mirza. *The Bible and the Quran: Biblical Figures in the Islamic Tradition*. Bloomsbury Academic, 2018.

Keriakos, Sandrine. "Apparitions of the Virgin in Egypt: Improving Relations Between Copts and Muslims?" In *Sharing Sacred Spaces in the Mediterranean*. Indiana University Press, 2012.

King, G. R. D. "The Paintings of the Pre-Islamic Kaʿba." *Muqarnas* 21 (2004): 219–229.

Knysh, Alexander. *Sufism: A New History of Islamic Mysticism*. Princeton University Press, 2017.

———. "Sufism and the Qur'an." In *Encyclopaedia of the Qur'ān*, edited by Johanna Pink. E. J. Brill, 2023.

Komurcu, Simge, and Özgür Saribas. "The Feeling of the Visitors Participating in Religious Tourism: The Case of Virgin Mary in Izmir." *International Journal of Contemporary Economics and Administrative Sciences* 6, no. 1–2 (2016): 31–42.

Krokus, Christian. *The Theology of Louis Massignon: Islam, Christ, and the Church*. The Catholic University of America Press, 2017.

Kronemer, Alex, director. *The Great Muslim American Road Trip*. PBS, 2022.

Lamptey, Jerusha Tanner. *Never Wholly Other: A Muslima Theology of Religious Pluralism*. Oxford University Press, 2014.

———. *Divine Words, Female Voices: Muslima Explorations in Comparative Feminist Theology*. Oxford University Press, 2018.

Lamya, H. *Hijab Butch Blues: A Memoir*. The Dial Press, 2023.

Levenson, Jon D. *Inheriting Abraham: The Legacy of the Patriarch in Judaism, Christianity, and Islam*. Princeton University Press, 2012.

Lings, Martin. *Muhammad: His Life Based on the Earliest Sources*. Inner Traditions, 2006.

———. *What Is Sufism?* George Allen and Unwin, 1975.

Madigan, Daniel. "Mary and Muhammad: Bearers of the Word." *Australasian Catholic Record* 80, no. 4 (2003): 417–427.

———. "Nostra Aetate and the Questions It Chose to Leave Open." *Gregorianum* 87, no. 4 (2006): 781–796.

Maunder, Chris, ed. *The Oxford Handbook of Mary*. Oxford University Press, 2019.

McAuliffe, J. D. "Chosen of All Women: Mary and Fatima in Qur'anic Exegesis." *Islamochristiana* 7 (1981): 19–28.

Mir, Mustansir. "The Sura as a Unity: A Twentieth Century Development in Qur'an Exegesis." In *Approaches to the Qur'an*, edited by G. R. Hawting and Abdul-kader A. Shareef. Routledge, 2003.

Mirza, Younus Y. "Abraham as an Iconoclast." *Islam and Christian–Muslim Relations* 16, no. 4 (2005): 413–428.

———. "Ishmael as Abraham's Sacrifice: Ibn Taymiyya and Ibn Kathir on the Intended Victim." *Islam and Christian–Muslim Relations* 24, no. 3 (2013): 277–298.

———. "Ibn Taymiyya as Exegete: Moses' Father-in-Law and the Messengers in Sūrat Yā Sīn." *Journal of Qur'anic Studies* 19 (2017): 39–71.

———. "The Islamic Mary: Between Prophecy and Orthodoxy." *Journal of Qur'anic Studies* 23, no. 3 (2021): 70–102.

Mourad, Suleiman A. "Christians and Christianity in the Sira of Muḥammad." In *Christian-Muslim Relations 600– 1500*, edited by David Thomas. E. J. Brill, 2021.

Mubarak, Hadia. "Women's Contemporary Readings of the Qur'an." In *The Routledge Companion to the Qur'an*, edited by George Archer, Maria Dakake, and Daniel Madigan. Routledge, 2022.

Nacim Pak-Shiraz. *Shi'i Islam in Iranian Cinema: Religion and Spirituality in Film*. I. B. Tauris, 2011.

Naguib, Shuruq. "Bint al-Shati's Approach to Tafsir: An Egyptian Exegete's Journey from Hermeneutics to Humanity." *Journal of Qur'anic Studies* 17, no. 1 (2015): 45–84.

Nasr, Seyyed Hossein, Caner K. Dagli, Maria Massi Dakake, Joseph E. B. Lumbard, and Mohammed Rustom, eds. *The Study Quran: A New Translation and Commentary*. Harper One, 2015.

Natif, Mika. "Images of the Virgin Mary in Mughal Art." *Khamseen: Islamic Art History Online*, March 28, 2024.

———. *Mughal Occidentalism: Artistic Encounters Between Europe and Asia at the Courts of India, 1580–1630*. Brill, 2018.

Neuwirth, Angelika. "Mary and Jesus: Counterbalancing the Biblical Patriarchs: A Re-Reading of Sūrat Maryam in Sūrat Āl ʿImrān (Q. 3:1–62)." In *Scripture, Poetry, and the Making of a Community: Reading the Qur'an as a Literary Text*, edited by Angelika Neuwirth. Oxford University Press, 2014.

———. *Studien zur Komposition der mekkanischen Suren: Die literarische Form des Koran— ein Zeugnis seiner Historizität?* 2nd ed. Walter de Gruyter, 2007.

Ozgur Alhassen, Leyla. *Quranic Stories: God, Revelation and the Audience*. Edinburgh University Press, 2021.

Peters, F. E. *The Children of Abraham: Judaism, Christianity, Islam*. Princeton University Press, 2004.

Pink, Johanna. "Translation." In *The Routledge Companion to the Qur'an*, edited by George Archer, Maria Dakake, and Daniel Madigan. Routledge, 2022.

Qureshi, Emran, and Michael Anthony Sells, eds. *The New Crusades: Constructing the Muslim Enemy*. Columbia University Press, 2003.

Qutb, Sayyid. *Fi zilal al-Qur'an*. 6 vols. Dar al-Sharuq, 2003.

Raven, Wim. *Some Early Islamic Texts on the Negus of Abyssinia*. Brill, 2021.

Reynolds, Gabriel Said. *The Qur'an and the Bible: Text and Commentary*. Yale University Press, 2018.

Rhodes, Jerusha Tanner. "Beyond the Rays of Truth? Nostra Aetate, Islam, and the Value of Difference." In *The Future of Interreligious Dialogue: A Multireligious Conversation on Nostra Aetate*, edited by C. L. Cohen, P. F. Knitter, and U. Rosenhagen. Orbis, 2017.

Ritter, H. "Djalal al-Din Rumi." In *Encyclopaedia of Islam*, 2nd ed., edited by P. Bearman, Th. Bianquis, C. E. Bosworth, E. van Donzel, and W. P. Heinrichs. E. J. Brill, 2012.

Robinson, Neal. "Jesus and Mary in the Qur'an: Some Neglected Affinities." *Religion* 20 (1990): 161–175.

Roded, Ruth. "Umm Salama Hind." In *Encyclopaedia of Islam*, 2nd ed., edited by P. Bearman, Th. Bianquis, C. E. Bosworth, E. van Donzel, and W. P. Heinrichs. E. J. Brill, 2021.

The Royal Aal Al-Bayt Institute for Islamic Thought. *A Common Word: Between Us and You*. Al Manhal, 2013.

Rumi, Jalal al-Din. *The Masnavi*, Book One. Translated by Jawid Mojaddedi. Oxford University Press, 2004.

———. *The Masnavi*, Book Two. Translated by Jawid Mojaddedi. Oxford University Press, 2007.

———. *The Masnavi*, Book Three. Translated by Jawid Mojaddedi. Oxford University Press, 2013.

Said, Yazid, and Lejla Demiri, eds. *The Future of Interfaith Dialogue: Muslim-Christian Encounters Through A Common Word*. Cambridge University Press, 2018.

Saritoprak, Zeki. "An Islamic Approach to Migration and Refugees." *CrossCurrents* 67, no. 3 (2017): 522–531.

———. "Mary in Islam." In *The Oxford Handbook of Mary*, edited by Chris Maunder. Oxford University Press, 2019.

Sayeed, Asma. *Women and the Transmission of Religious Knowledge in Islam*. Cambridge University Press, 2013.

Schimmel, Annemarie. *My Soul Is a Woman: The Feminine in Islam*. Continuum, 1997.

———. *Mystical Dimensions of Islam*. University of North Carolina Press, 1975.

Schleifer, Aliah. *Mary the Blessed Virgin of Islam*. Fons Vitae, 2008.

Sells, Michael. *Early Islamic Mysticism: Sufi, Qur'an, Miraj, Poetic and Theological Writings*. Paulist Press, 1996.

Shavit, Uriya. "Europe, the New Abyssinia: On the Role of the First Hijra in the Fiqh al-Aqalliyyat al-Muslima Discourse." *Islam and Christian–Muslim Relations* 29, no. 3 (2018): 371–391.

Silvers, Laury. "Early Pious, Mystic Sufi Women." In *The Cambridge Companion to Sufism*, edited by Lloyd Ridgeon. Cambridge University Press, 2015.

Shaw, Wendy. "The Islam in Islamic Art History: Secularism and Public Discourse." *Journal of Art Historiography* 6 (2012): 1–34.

Stowasser, Barbara. "Mary." In *Encyclopaedia of the Qur'ān*, edited by Jane Dammen McAuliffe. E. J. Brill, 2001.

*The Sublime Quran*. Translated by Laleh Bakhtiar. Kazi Publications, 2007.

Sulami, Muhammad ibn al-Husayn Cornell. *Early Sufi Women: Dhikr an-Niswa al-Muta'abbidat as Sufiyyat*. Translated by Rkia Cornell. Fons Vitae, 1999.

Tahawi, Ahmad ibn Muhammad. *The Creed of Imam al-Tahawi*. Translated by Hamza Hanson Yusuf. Zaytuna Institute, 2007.

Tatari, Muna, and Klaus von Stosch. *Mary in the Qur'an: Friend of God, Virgin, Mother*. Translated by Peter Lewis. Gingko, 2021.

Thomas, David. "Miracles in Islam." In *The Cambridge Companion to Miracles*, edited by Graham H. Twelftree. Cambridge University Press, 2011.

Thurlkill, Mary. *Chosen Among Women: Mary and Fatima in Medieval Christianity and Shiite Islam*. University of Notre Dame Press, 2007.

Tompkins, Ptolemy. "Rumi Rules!" *Time Magazine*, October 29, 2002.

Toorawa, Shawkat. "Surat Maryam (Q. 19): Lexicon, Lexical Echoes, English Translation." *Journal of Qur'anic Studies* 13, no. 1 (2011): 25–78.

Valkenberg, Wilhelmus G. B. M. "A Faithful Christian Interpretation of Islam." In *Faithful Interpretations: Truth and Islam in Catholic Theology of Religions*, edited by Philip Geister and Gösta Hallonsten. The Catholic University of America Press, 2021.

von Stosch, Klaus. "Mary and Her Role in the Qur'an." In *Mary in the Qur'an: Friend of God, Virgin, Mother.* Translated by Peter Lewis. Gingko, 2021.

Wadud, Amina. *Inside the Gender Jihad: Women's Reform in Islam.* Oneworld, 2006.

Watt, Montgomery. "Ibn Hisham." In *Encyclopaedia of Islam.* 2nd ed., edited by P. Bearman, Th. Bianquis, C. E. Bosworth, E. van Donzel, and W. P. Heinrichs. E. J. Brill, 2021.

Weddle, David. *Miracles: Wonder and Meaning in World Religions.* New York University Press, 2010.

Wensinck, A. J. "ʿAmr b. al-ʿAs." In *Encyclopaedia of Islam*, 2nd ed., edited by P. Bearman, Th. Bianquis, C. E. Bosworth, E. van Donzel, and W. P. Heinrichs. E. J. Brill, 2021.

———. "Muʿdjiza." In *Encyclopaedia of Islam.* 2nd ed., edited by P. Bearman, Th. Bianquis, C. E. Bosworth, E. van Donzel, and W. P. Heinrichs. E. J. Brill, 2012.

———. *The Muslim Creed: Its Genesis and Historical Development.* Cambridge University Press, 1932.

Westbrook, Donald A. "Our Lady of Zeitoun (1968–1971): Egyptian Mariophanies in Historical, Interfaith, and Ecumenical Context." *Nova Religio: The Journal of Alternative and Emergent Religions* 21, no. 2 (2017): 85–99.

Williams, Alan. "The Visitation of Mary and Rumi's Comments on the Nature of Story: Mathnawi, Book Two." *Mawlana Rumi Review* 6 (2015): 119–127.

Willy, Jansen. "Visions of Mary in the Middle East: Gender and the Power of a Symbol." In *Gender, Religion and Change in the Middle East: Two Hundred Years of History*, edited by Inger Marie Okkenhaug and Ingvild Flaskerud. Bloomsbury, 2005.

Xavier, Merin Shobhana. "Gendering the Divine: Women, Femininity, and Queer Identities on the Sufi Path." In *The Routledge Handbook of Islam and Gender*, edited by Justine Howe. Routledge, 2021.

Yazbeck Haddad, Yvonne, and Jane I. Smith. "The Quest for 'A Common Word': Initial Christian Responses to a Muslim Initiative." *Islam and Christian–Muslim Relations* 20, no. 4 (2009): 369–388.

Yazicioglu, Isra. "Redefining the Miraculous: al-Ghazali, Ibn Rushd, and Said Nursi on Qur'an and Miracles." *Journal of Qur'anic Studies* 13, no. 2 (2011): 86–108.

of Religion, edited by Philip [illegible] and [illegible]. The Catholic University of America Press, 2021.

van Reeth, Jan M. F. "Mary and Her Role in the Qur'an." In [illegible]. Translated by [illegible] Lewis. [illegible], 2016.

Wadud, Amina. Inside the Gender Jihad: Women's Reform in Islam. Oneworld, 2006.

Watt, W. Montgomery. "Ibn Hishām." In Encyclopaedia of Islam, 2nd ed., edited by P. Bearman, Th. Bianquis, C. E. Bosworth, E. van Donzel, and W. P. Heinrichs. E. J. Brill, 2012.

[illegible], Daniel. [illegible]. New York University Press, 2016.

Wensinck, A. J. "Amina." In Encyclopaedia of Islam, 2nd ed., edited by P. Bearman, Th. Bianquis, C. E. Bosworth, E. van Donzel, and W. P. Heinrichs. E. J. Brill, 2012.

———. "Maryam." In Encyclopaedia of Islam, 2nd ed., edited by P. Bearman, Th. Bianquis, C. E. Bosworth, E. van Donzel, and W. P. Heinrichs. E. J. Brill, 2012.

———. The Muslim Creed: Its Genesis and Historical Development. Cambridge University Press, 1932.

Westbrook, Donald A. "Our Lady of Zeitoun (1968–1971): Egyptian Marian Apparitions in Historical, Interfaith, and Ecumenical Context." Nova Religio: The Journal of Alternative and Emergent Religions 21, no. 1 (2017): [illegible].

[illegible], Alan. "The Visitation of Mary and [illegible] Comments on the Nature [illegible] of Mary [illegible] Book Two." [illegible] (2015): 159–[illegible].

[illegible]. "Visions of Mary in the Middle East: Guardian of the Power of a Symbol." In Gender, Religion and Change in the Middle East: Two Hundred Years of History, edited by Inger Marie Okkenhaug and Ingvild Flaskerud. Bloomsbury, 2005.

[illegible]. "Understanding the Divine: Women, Femininity and Queer Identity in the Sufi Path." In The Routledge Handbook of Islam and Gender, edited by Justine Howe. Routledge, 2021.

Yazbeck Haddad, Yvonne, and Jane I. Smith. "The Quest for 'A Common Word': Initial Christian Responses to a Muslim Initiative." Islam and Christian–Muslim Relations 20, no. 4 (2009): 369–388.

Yazicioglu, Isra. "Redefining the Miraculous: al-Ghazali, Ibn Rushd and Said Nursi on Qur'anic Miracle Stories." Journal of Qur'anic Studies 13, no. 2 (2011): 86–108.

# INDEX OF SUBJECTS AND NAMES

Praise for *The Islamic Mary*

This book presents an engaging exploration of the figure of Mary/Maryam in Islamic sources and Muslim culture. The work has incredible range, examining Maryam's presence in Muslim scripture, religious literature, theology, and mysticism. It also elucidates the connections between Maryam and a host of other female sacred figures in Muslim culture, from Fatima to Rabi'a. Drawing on a wealth of primary and secondary literature, this book offers a truly comprehensive portrait of the Islamic Mary, while making a compelling case for her importance for contemporary interreligious understanding, especially among the Abrahamic faiths.

Maria M. Dakake, associate professor of religious studies, George Mason University

Younus Y. Mirza's *The Islamic Mary* is an outstanding book that will be welcomed by Muslims and Christians alike. Mirza's well-written, well-documented, and engaging book provides a multifaceted and in-depth study of the significant role that the Virgin Mary plays in the Qur'an, Muslim history, tradition, scholarship, and Islamic art.

John L. Esposito, Distinguished University Professor Emeritus and founding director of the Prince Alwaleed bin Talal Center for Muslim-Christian Understanding, Georgetown University; and author of *Islam: The Straight Path*

In this slim volume, author Younus Mirza walks us through portrayals of Mary found in Islamic scripture, prophetic literature, mysticism, art, film, and the present day, offering readers a fresh look at the Muslim Maryam that is engaging and accessible.

Rita George-Tvrtković, consultor, Vatican Dicastery for Interreligious Dialogue, and author of *Christians, Muslims, and Mary: A History*

Younus Mirza's *The Islamic Mary* is a groundbreaking exploration of Maryam's legacy, blending cutting-edge scholarship with personal insight to appeal to both religious studies scholars and general readers. The work examines Mary's enduring and novel roles in Islamic thought, devotion, and mysticism—spanning Qur'anic accounts and feminist scholarship—all while illuminating connections with Christian theology. This comprehensive, accessible survey highlights Mary's significance across centuries, from early Muslim texts to contemporary interfaith dialogue.

Celene Ibrahim, author of *Women and Gender in the Qur'an*

Younus Mirza's *The Islamic Mary* provides one of the most comprehensive and compelling overviews of Mary's representation in the Qur'an, prophetic tradition, medieval Islamic scholarship, and contemporary literature. Grounded in research from a wide variety of genres, this book is essential reading for anyone who seeks an accurate understanding of Mary and her significance to Muslim communities.

Hadia Mubarak, associate professor of religion,
Queens University of Charlotte

This outstanding study offers one of the most thorough examinations to date of the figure of Mary in the Islamic tradition. Deeply researched and clearly presented, it is poised to become a definitive reference on Islamic conceptions of Mary for years to come.

Feryal Salem, associate professor of Arabic and Islamic
Studies, American Islamic College